DOING
DISCOURSE
RESEARCH

SAGE has been part of the global academic community since 1965, supporting high quality research and learning that transforms society and our understanding of individuals, groups, and cultures. SAGE is the independent, innovative, natural home for authors, editors and societies who share our commitment and passion for the social sciences.

Find out more at: **www.sagepublications.com**

Connect, Debate, Engage on Methodspace

Connect with other researchers and discuss your research interests

Keep up with announcements in the field, for example calls for papers and jobs

Discover and review resources

Engage with featured content such as key articles, podcasts and videos

Find out about relevant conferences and events

Connecting the Research Community

www.methodspace.com

brought to you by

DOING DISCOURSE RESEARCH

An Introduction for Social Scientists

Reiner Keller

Translated by
Bryan Jenner

Los Angeles | London | New Delhi
Singapore | Washington DC

Los Angeles | London | New Delhi
Singapore | Washington DC

SAGE Publications Ltd
1 Oliver's Yard
55 City Road
London EC1Y 1SP

SAGE Publications Inc.
2455 Teller Road
Thousand Oaks, California 91320

SAGE Publications India Pvt Ltd
B 1/I 1 Mohan Cooperative Industrial Area
Mathura Road
New Delhi 110 044

SAGE Publications Asia-Pacific Pte Ltd
3 Church Street
#10-04 Samsung Hub
Singapore 049483

Originally published in German as *Diskursforschung* by
VS Verlag fur Sozialwissenschaften, Wiesbaden 2007
First published in English by SAGE 2013
© Reiner Keller 2013

Editor: Katie Metzler
Assistant editor: Anna Horvai
Production editor: Ian Antcliff
Translator: Bryan Jenner
Copyeditor: Jennifer Hinchliffe
Proofreader: Anna Gilding
Marketing manager: Ben Griffin-Sherwood
Cover design: Lisa Harper
Typeset by: C&M Digitals (P) Ltd, Chennai,
India
Printed and bound by: CPI Group (UK) Ltd,
Croydon, CR0 4YY

Library of Congress Control Number: 2012939245

British Library Cataloguing in Publication data

A catalogue record for this book is available from
the British Library

MIX
Paper from
responsible sources
FSC
www.fsc.org   FSC® C013604

ISBN 978-1-4462-4970-3
ISBN 978-1-4462-4971-0 (pbk)

Contents

About the author

Reiner Keller studied sociology at the universities of Saarbrücken, Bamberg and Rennes (France). After working as a social scientist, he got a PhD in sociology at the Technical University Munich in 1997. From 1997–2006 he taught sociology at Augsburg University where he passed his 'Habilitation'. In 2007 he was appointed a full professorship in sociology at Landau University; since late 2011 he is holder of a Chair in Sociology at Augsburg University. His main interests are in the domains of discourse theory and research, sociology of knowledge and culture, and qualitative methodologies. He has extensively published in these areas. Among his latest books are *The Sociology of Knowledge Approach to Discourse SKAD* (2005, 3rd edition; translation in preparation for 2013), *Michel Foucault* (2008), *The Interpretative Paradigm* (2012). In 2011, his approach to discourse (SKAD) was published in the journal *Human Studies*. In 2012, he contributed to an issue of *Qualitative Sociology Review*.

ONE

The Current Relevance of
Discourse Research

Preamble

Since this Introduction to Discourse Research first appeared in 2003 the field of the social science analysis of discourse has grown enormously and the number of approaches has also expanded. This seems to be especially true in the German-speaking world: here the recent boom in discourse research appears much more marked than in English or French speaking contexts. Evidence for this may be found in the recent appearance of a number of book series, survey works, networks, and a plethora of conferences, online journals and web-platforms as well as the countless monographs and collections that we cannot acknowledge fully in this short introduction. One of the most important trends of the past decade has certainly been the marked expansion of discourse research within linguistics, building bridges to the social sciences, together with the increasing interest in questions of the analysis of audio-visual data or multimodal data formats. If one compares the older and the more recent editions of some German introductions to Critical Discourse Analysis or Historical Discourse Analysis, it is possible to speak of a tendency towards the 'sociologizing of discourse research' and as such a clear indicator for the approach contained in the present book.

Collective Orders of Knowledge and Discourses

In the social sciences there is a basic agreement that the relationship between human beings and the world are mediated by means of collectively created symbolic meaning systems or orders of knowledge. The different paradigms differ according to the theoretical, methodological and empirical value they attach to this assessment. In analyses of the social significance of knowledge and symbolic orders, in recent years, the terms *discourse, discourse theory* and *Discourse Analysis* have gained enormously in importance. This is particularly true of the large-scale reception of the works of Michel Foucault. To a considerably smaller extent the claim may also be made of developments within the interpretative paradigm (located in sociology). The boom in discourse-oriented theories and research may be witnessed on an impressive scale in various disciplines in the social sciences and humanities, for example in history, linguistics, literary studies, education and politics, or in sociology. Reference to the term 'discourse' occurs when theoretical perspectives and research questions relate to the constitution and construction of the world in the concrete use of signs and the underlying structural patterns or rules for the production of meaning. Discourses may be understood as more or less successful attempts to stabilize, at least temporarily, attributions of meaning and orders of interpretation, and thereby to institutionalize a collectively binding order of knowledge in a social ensemble. Discourse theories or discourse analyses, on the other hand, are scientific endeavours designed to investigate the processes implied here: social sciences' discourse research is concerned with the relationship between speaking/writing as activity or social practices and the (re)production of meaning systems/orders of knowledge, the social actors involved in this, the rules and resources underlying these processes, and their consequences in social collectivities.

Discourse theories and discourse analyses differ in their reference to the use of language or signs from other treatments of language in the social sciences, such as the sociology of language, or the ethnomethodologically based conversation analysis, because these are neither interested in social-structural formations in linguistic usage nor in linguistic usage as a form or performance of action. And unlike Jürgen Habermas's *Discourse Ethics* (Habermas 1991a), which has sometimes also been labelled a discourse theory, it is not a matter of formulating ideal conditions for processes of argumentation.[1] What is at the heart of the perspective on social science Discourse Analysis presented here is more the analysis of institutional regulations of declarative practices and their performative and reality-constituting power. While *discourse theories* develop general theoretical perspectives on the linguistic constitution of meaningfulness of reality, *discourse analyses* concentrate on the empirical investigation of discourses. The term Discourse Analysis, however, does not refer to any specific method, but rather to a *research perspective* on particular research objects that are understood as discourses. What this means, in concrete terms, in relation to research questions and translation into methodological practice, depends on the disciplinary and theoretical background. The concept of discourse is therefore related, within the narrower field of discourse research, to different phenomena, and heterogeneous research goals are connected with its use. Discourse theories and discourse analyses are mostly understood today as qualitative, hermeneutic or interpretative perspectives or are attributed to these categories in methodological survey treatments (Hitzler and Honer 1997; Flick 2009). Despite the heterogeneity of approaches in discourse theory and Discourse Analysis, four features may be taken as the lowest common denominators in the use of the term discourse. Discourse theories and discourse analyses:

- are concerned with the actual use of (written or spoken) language and other symbolic forms in social practices;
- emphasize that in the practical use of signs, meanings of phenomena are socially constructed and these phenomena are thereby constituted in their social reality;
- claim that individual instances of interpretation may be understood as parts of a more comprehensive discourse structure that is temporarily produced and stabilized by specific institutional-organizational contexts; and
- assume that the use of symbolic orders is subject to rules of interpretation and action that may be reconstructed.

For discourse research, with its base in the social sciences and its focus on the institutional regulation of collective orders of knowledge, the structure and practice-oriented theoretical views of Pierre Bourdieu (1990a) and Anthony Giddens (1986) are important. Giddens, for example, understands

---

[1]On *Discourse Analysis* see Chapter 2.2 and Brown and Yule (1983), Gee (2010).

action (and therefore also communicative action) analogously to Ludwig Wittgenstein's theory of language games as realizations of structural patterns (rules); these exist in the concrete performance of an action which actualizes them, confirms them in their validity and projects them further, but which is also able to question, undermine or transform them. The actual event is thus not a direct consequence of the underlying structures but a result of the actively interpreting interaction between social actors and these patterns. For this reason concrete language usage differs in its possibilities for world (re)interpretation, from the rigid systems of structuralism (see Chapter 2.1).

It would be too hasty to derive the growing interest in discourse-theoretical and discourse-analytical perspectives solely from science-internal processes. Indeed, here there is also an expression of the scientific reflexion of heterogeneous social changes and processes of transformation that in recent times have been given the label *knowledge society*, whose importance for the development of modern societies has been stressed, for example, by Giddens (1991). With the increase in systematic knowledge production, public awareness of the contingency of this knowledge has also grown. This is why Helga Nowotny has indicated that facts lose their unambiguity, that is their unambiguous classifiability (Nowotny 1999). Similarly, in other areas of social studies of science and technology, an increase in hybrid phenomena has been observed, and these cannot be unambiguously attributed to nature, society or technology (Latour 1993). It is precisely for this reason that discourses are of high social importance as processes and as attempts at attributing and stabilizing meaning. Apart from the exponential growth in the production of knowledge there is a second empirical reason for the boom in discourse research: the enormous expansion in professionalized communication processes and technologies, that is, the strategic and instrumental processing of linguistic practice in the most varied realms of social action (Keller 2005a).

TWO

Approaches in Discourse Research

The term 'discourse', in everyday English, means a simple conversation, an interchange between different people. In French or other Romance languages *discours* (or *discorso*) is the usual term for a 'learnéd speech', a lecture, a treatise, sermon, presentation and more besides. Talking of 'public or political discourses' in both languages refers to debates in the public (political sphere), mediated by mass media. This latter usage, which also has been turning up for a number of years in everyday German, mostly characterizes a subject and process of public discussion (e.g. the debate on university reform), a specific chain of argument (e.g. the 'neoliberal discourse') or the point of view or utterances of a politician, a trade union representative (e.g. talking of 'Trade Union Discourse'), and so on, in the course of a current debate. It is now also being used in organized processes of discussion and deliberation. However, 'discourse' is much more widely used as a non-technical term in English and French, and its academic currency is largely due to this kind of understanding of the term. Here, 'discourse' is also understood in the social sciences and humanities in widely differing ways. This is both true of its theoretical conceptualization in respect of the research interests of a particular discipline and also its methodological implementation in concrete research projects. In recent years, particularly in the English-speaking world, there have been many introductory and survey treatments of the term *discourse*. They demonstrate the enormous expansion of discourse-related perspectives in a range of disciplines and also across disciplinary boundaries. Several series of publications and journals, such as *Discourse and Society*, or *Discourse Studies*, but also workshops, conferences and summer schools, have been established as forums for relevant discussions. From a trans-disciplinary viewpoint it is also possible to distinguish a range of different emphases. The most important basic ideas will be exemplified below. But first I should like to examine briefly the academic history of the term *discourse*.

2.1 The History of the Term 'Discourse'

The linguistic roots of 'discourse' are to be found in classical Latin *discurrere* or *discursus*. As an everyday word the term has been used in a variety of contexts. In the thirteenth century more specific philosophical versions arose, and from the sixteenth century onwards it was frequently used to characterize 'learnéd treatises' (Schalk 1997/98; Nennen 2000a; Kohlhaas 2000). In the context of Philosophical Pragmatism, Charles S. Peirce and George H. Mead (Mead 1934:89) use the expression 'universe of discourse.' This comes very close to the present-day use of the term in the sense of this introduction: '(…) a universe of discourse is simply a system of common or shared meanings' (Mead 1934: 89). In this respect the term discourse refers to the link between an individual linguistic event and a context-dependent meaning attribution: signs are only meaningful in the context of more comprehensive language games.

In American Structural Linguistics and Distributional Linguistics, Zellig Harris introduced the term 'Discourse Analysis' in 1952 to characterize his approach to a structural-grammatical analysis of Native American languages; 'discourse' here refers to supra-sentential linguistic structures (Harris 1952). Under this label there developed a broad spectrum of linguistic-pragmatic research, particularly of processes of oral communication. Harris's suggestions became a source of inspiration for quantitative analyses of major text corpora at the interface between linguistics and history (Guilhaumou 2006).

For the use of the term discourse in the sense used in this introduction, the theoretical-conceptual developments in French Structuralism and Post-structuralism after the mid-1950s were of major importance. They can be outlined here with reference to only a few key words.[1] In France in the 1950s and 60s, 'structuralism' was used to refer to a set of theories and research projects in a variety of disciplines, which shared a reliance on the linguistic theory of Ferdinand de Saussure (1965). After the mid-1960s, as a result of the dispute with a range of critiques, a number of structuralists

---

[1]See Dosse (1997, 1998a), Williams (1999).

then developed modified positions that are referred to as Neo-structuralism or Post-structuralism. Whereas Structuralism understood and investigated discourses as abstract and objective rule-systems, Post-structuralism turned its attention more strongly to the interaction between (abstract) symbolic orders and the concrete use of language or signs, that is, the relationship of structures and events (mostly linguistic actions or social practices).

At the onset of the development of Structuralism we find first and foremost the reception conveyed by the ethnologist Claude Lévi-Strauss of the linguistic theory of the Genevan linguist Ferdinand de Saussure in French social sciences and humanities.[2] Saussure developed a scientific concept of language which takes this to be a system of signs – 'la langue' – which underlies concrete speaking and writing, that is the individual's practical use of language.[3] This linguistic system is understood as an historically developed social institution – comparable to a political system or law, the genesis of which can be traced back to linguistic interactions within a speech community. Of course, this is an emergent phenomenon that has arisen as a whole out of the totality of individual utterances, without being identical to them. It is no coincidence that this description is reminiscent of the sociology of Emile Durkheim:

'The sociological scope of the language/speech concept is obvious. The manifest affinity of the language according to Saussure and of Durkheim's conception of a collective consciousness independent of its individual manifestations has been emphasised very early on. A direct influence of Durkheim on Saussure has even been postulated, it has been alleged that Saussure had followed very closely the debate between Durkheim and Tarde and that his conception of the language came from Durkheim while that of speech was a kind of concession to Tarde's idea on the individual element.' (Barthes 1967: 23 [1964])

---

[2]More recent discussions of 'social semiotics', discourse research or the sociological interpretative paradigm emphasize, following Charles Peirce, George Herbert Mead, Charles W. Morris or (more recently) Umberto Eco, the 'conventional' character of signs, i.e. the social agreement on their meaning and the social embedding of their usage (see Meier 2008, 2011; Keller 2005a; Keller 2009).

[3]That Saussure in fact insisted much more on language in use has been revealed by recent research (Jäger, L. 2010; Schneider 2008). Saussure views language as the most important system of signs; but these considerations can, by analogy, be transferred to other systems of signs. In this sense, in semiotics all cultural processes are seen as communication processes, i.e. processes of the release and reception of signs. On this, and also on the common features and differences between the language theories of Saussure and Peirce, see, for example, Eco (1978), Chandler (2002: 17ff); Schneider (2008).

To speak of language as a system is to imply the assumption of certain relationships, regularities or structures between the elements in the system; these function as a code to govern the practical use of language. What is very important here for the development of Discourse Analysis perspectives is the definitive rejection of a representational perspective, that is, the idea that the sound pattern and meaning of a sign are a reflection of the empirical phenomenon to which it relates.[4] According to Saussure the value of a sign results from its status in the sign-system of the *langue,* that is to say, in the relationships to the other signs from which it differs. In this sense it is random or 'arbitrary' because it has no extralinguistic or natural necessity; not in the sense that one could use signs at random in speaking, for then no understanding would be possible. The model of Saussure that we have presented here in a small number of its essential features was applied by Claude Lévi-Strauss at the end of the 1940s to questions in ethnology and anthropology. Concrete cultural phenomena, such as relationships within families or the narration of myths, are taken by him, in analogy to Saussurean linguistics, as instances of *parole,* that is, as events which have an underlying subject-independent rule-system, for example a system of relationship-structures or a system of myths (that is: a type of *langue*). In the same way as signs in the language system, the individual elements here create their value or meaning through their delimiting relationships within this systemic structure. The task of any science is then to reconstruct these systems of objective structures for their particular research objects.

To account for the current vogue of the term 'discourse', the works of the philosopher Michel Foucault have been the most successful.[5] In 1966, in a context of structuralist élan, he published his analysis of *Les mots et les choses* (*The Order of Things,* Foucault 1991c). In this, looking back over the Renaissance, Enlightenment, Romanticism and Modernism, he distinguishes specific types of basic knowledge or general epistemological

---

[4]Saussure is not alone here: the representative function of language is also rejected, for example, in the work of Nietzsche, Wittgenstein, Heidegger and in American Pragmatism. Similar positions can also be traced back to Plato (Dosse 1998a: 43; Rorty 1967, 1979, 1989).

[5]Indeed there was a surge of (today less well-known) discourse-related work in France in the late 1960s (including Michel Pêcheux and others) which cannot be discussed here (but see below Chapter 2.3).

structures (called 'the episteme') that appear in succession and supersede one another. Just as *langue* underlies *parole* and makes it possible, so do these epistemological structures underlie concrete epistemological activities and their linguistic fixation in the widest possible range of academic disciplines. In this way Foucault – like Friedrich Nietzsche and his own teacher, the historian of science, Georges Canguilhem before him – dismisses all ideas of a continual development of scientific knowledge throughout history in the sense of a constantly progressing discovery of truth. This book, characterized by its subtitle as an 'Archaeology of the Humanities',

> 'is the publishing event of the year and the summer blockbuster (...). Michel Foucault was borne along by the structuralist tide and his work came to embody the philosophical synthesis of the new thinking that had been developing for fifteen years. If the author later put some distance between himself and the structuralist tag, which he considered insulting, in 1966 he considered himself to be at the heart of the phenomenon.' (Dosse 1998a: 330)

The spread of Structuralist assumptions that we have only hinted at here was subjected from the outset to criticism in France from Paul Ricoeur, Julia Kristeva, Jacques Derrida and many others.[6] The objections were based on phenomenological-hermeneutic traditions in philosophy, the Semiotics of American Pragmatism, linguistic-philosophical reflections of actual language use and alternative scientific theories of human linguistic competence. In particular, objections were raised against three features of the Structuralist perspective: firstly there was criticism of its scientific objectivism, which was rated as exaggerated, and of the ahistoric nature and missing dynamic of structural models. An example of this is Foucault's description of the epoch-specific and discontinuous juxtaposition of different orders of knowledge that accompany the explicit rejection of questions concerning the reason and manner of their change. The second set of objections was directed at the lack of any concern – in favour of the preference for structures – with the concrete use of language, that is, with single communicative events. According to this view Structuralism is only concerned with abstract systems of difference, without being able to show how these underlie concrete phenomena. Thirdly, and finally, there was criticism of the

---

[6]See, for example, Dosse (1997).

missing reflection of the meaning dimension of symbolic orders and their application in the interpretative behaviour of social actors, that is, the processes of social conventionalization, the handling and reinterpretation of actual uses of signs. In Structuralism, for example, abstractions are made from the authorship of text-producers and the interpretative behaviour of recipients, if it is a matter of the meaning carried by texts, because behind this, it is assumed, there lies concealed the abstract structure of the *langue* in question. In contrast, Reception Aesthetics refers to the possibility in principle of infinitely different modes of textual reading by historically based individual interpreters. While these and other critical voices initially gained only occasional attention, their influence changed at the end of the 1960s, not least in the context of the student unrest of 1968, where there was a heated and polemical argument as to whether it was Structures or people that took to the streets (Dosse 1997: 122ff). Many scholars working in a variety of disciplines and more or less shaped by Structuralism, such as Roland Barthes, Michel Foucault, Pierre Bourdieu, Louis Althusser or Jacques Lacan, have attempted to incorporate arguments from critiques of Structuralism into their theories and to examine more closely questions of the real practical use of symbol systems. This led them to develop neo- or post-structuralist approaches. Questions about the relationship of structures and events, actions and subjects, static and dynamic states are thus dealt with in a variety of ways.[7]

Interlude: The Discourse Ethics of Jürgen Habermas and Discourse Research

One of the most frequent uses of the term discourse was triggered by the *Discourse Ethics* developed by the German social philosopher Jürgen Habermas, and now also viewed as a discourse theory (e.g. Habermas 1985, 1991a, 1997; Finlayson 2005, Nennen 2000; Gottschalk-Mazouz 2000). As a reaction to a variety of linguistic and social science theories, Habermas develops, on the basis of the tradition of critical theory, a comprehensive

---

[7]The diagnosis given by Dosse (1998b) of the French debate is that there was a 'complete return to the reference to actor and subject' from the beginning of the 1970s.

'theory of communicative action.' In this the idea of 'dominance-free discourse' plays a major role. A core idea is the assumption that human linguistic ability or competence implies exactly four design requirements which are carried in every seriously intended concrete speech action of a linguistically competent and rational speaker and which must be mutually assumed by the participants within the communication. It is only in this way that linguistic understanding is at all possible. Thus, we expect that statements will be intelligible and true, that the speaker will show truthfulness, and that what is uttered will be correct. These properties – in the opinion of Habermas – can be used in a targeted way in the form of 'discourses'. 'Discourses' in this sense are continuations of normal communicative action by different means, namely organized (discussion) processes of argumentative debate and deliberation. By means of explicit rules and structuring measures they are expected to ensure the broadest possible adherence to the above-mentioned claims to validity; this is also true of the possibility of participation/speaking for all those who are 'touched' by the subject in question. Discourse Ethics formulates a normative model based on social and linguistic philosophy, but not a research programme. Habermas's approach has therefore little to do with discourse research; admittedly his concept of discourse has been partially invoked in the context of Critical Discourse Analysis as a critical measure for the assessment of the 'degree of distortion' in real processes of communication (see Chapter 2.4). For example the Austrian critical discourse analyst Ruth Wodak uses Discourse Ethics as a measure for determining empirically – against the ideal model – distortions or disturbances in 'real discourses', that is, in the course of real conversations. Discourse Ethics becomes here a normative basis of critical discourse linguistic research, which investigates 'Disorders of Discourse' in institutional contexts and organizational settings (Wodak 1996). In contrast, the reference in the Discourse Analysis research of Jürgen Gerhards et al. (see Chapter 2.5) is quite different. These aim to show empirically, using reconstructions of public discussion processes on contentious topics (such as abortion) from the mass media, that the modern mass-mediated public sphere does not correspond to Habermas's discourse ideal. In this sense Discourse Ethics does not serve as a normative benchmark for critique, but rather it is shown empirically that processes of public discussion do not adhere to the ideal of a regulative idea (e.g. Ferree, Gamson, Gerhards and Rucht 2002; Gerhards 2010)

Introductory Literature on the Term Discourse

The general background to the perspectives on discourse research consist of debates of 'Social Science Constructivism' and 'Sociology of Knowledge' (Burr 1997; Hacking 2000; Gergen 1999; McCarthy 1996; Power 2000; Knoblauch 2005b). On Discourse Research there are many introductions, surveys and collections that mostly present particular emphases in either Discourse Theory or in Discourse Analysis (DA). More recently there have also been proposals for disseminating these perspectives. From these many introductions, let me list a few that seem to me to be very helpful. Further literature on the particular approaches will be presented later.

MacDonell (1986) explains discourse theory developments from Structuralism and Pêcheux's Marxist Discourse Analysis down to the works of Foucault; Bublitz (2003) accounts for Foucauldian perspectives on discourse; Mills (1997) provides an introduction to the works of Foucault and creates references to feminist and post-colonialist discussions; Howarth (2000) outlines developments from Saussure, Althusser, Foucault and Post-structuralism down to the discourse theory of Mouffe and Laclau. Paltridge (2007) presents varied approaches to discourse from linguistics to critical Discourse Analysis. Landwehr (2009) gives an introduction to the bases of Discourse Historical approaches. The contributions in Keller, Hirseland, Schneider and Viehöver (2011; 2010) present theoretical and conceptual proposals and practical applications in research from a variety of disciplines. In Keller, Hirseland, Schneider and Viehöver (2005) relations and differences between sociology of knowledge and post-structuralist perspectives in discourse research are discussed. Van Dijk (1997a, b), Parker and The Bolton Discourse Network (1999) describe procedures in DA from a broad spectrum of disciplines; Wetherell, Taylor and Yates (2001b) present examples of the application of DA; Gee (1999, 2010) relates DA with considerations in Discourse Theory. Jørgensen and Philipps (2002), in addition to the Discourse Theory of Laclau and Mouffe, also present Critical Discourse Analysis and Discursive Psychology (Potter, Wetherell et al.), and seek an integration of these approaches. Andersen (2003) undertakes a comparison of the analytical strategies of discourse theory, conceptual history and system theory. The *Readers* by Wetherell, Taylor and Yates (2001a) and Jaworski and Coupland (2006) present, in particular, a selection of foundation texts, but not only from the context of DA. Philipps and Hardy (2002) provide a concise overview of theoretical bases and practical applications of a kind of Discourse Research that seeks to combine Discourse Theory and DA. Williams (1999), Charaudeau and Maingueneau (2002) and Guilhaumou (2006) document the development and status of French discourse research. Widdowson (2007) provides a concentrated insight into discourse-linguistic questions. Wodak and Krzyzanowski

(2008) introduce analytical strategies against a linguistic background, taking into account various media genres. Bührmann and Schneider (2008) argue for a dispositive type of research; in this discourse concepts and discourse-related questions would continue to play a major role.[8]

2.2 Discourse Analysis

The collective term Discourse Analysis designates many different research approaches that are concerned with the analysis of 'natural' communication processes in different contexts, and from linguistic, sociolinguistic, ethnomethodological-conversation-analysis, sociological and psychological perspectives. In this we are dealing with the most widespread variant of the term discourse in English discourse literature.[9] Even if Conversation Analysis (Psathas 1995; Ten Have 2007; Hutchby and Wooffitt 1988) might be added to the spectrum of DA, questions of communicative context and updated content play a more important role here. This is demonstrated in particular in Critical Discourse Analysis that will be dealt with below (see Chapter 2.4)

To the Dutch linguist Teun van Dijk, Discourse Analysis refers to an approach which aims – across disciplinary boundaries – at analysing language use in speaking or writing as a factual process happening in a social context: 'text and talk in action'. In this the concept of context extends from local-situational to macro-social and historically far-reaching diachronic or synchronic dimensions. The determination of the beginning and end of a discourse is carried out following the research question. Important questions are concerned with who uses language in a communicative event, how, why and when:

'I have characterized discourse as essentially involving three main dimensions, namely language use, cognition, and interaction in their sociocultural contexts. Instead of vaguely summarizing, paraphrasing or quoting discourse, as is still often the case in social scientific approaches, discourse analytical studies distinguish various levels,

---

[8]Literary discussions are to be found in Fohrmann and Müller (1988), Bogdal (1999).

[9]The contributions in the journals *Discourse and Society* and *Discourse Studies* are mostly concerned with this.

units or constructs within each of these dimensions, and formulate the rules and strategies of their normative or actual uses. They functionally relate such units or levels among each other, and thereby also explain *why* they are being used. In the same way, they functionally connect discourse structures with social and cultural context structures, and both again to the structures and strategies of cognition. *Discourse Analysis* thus moves from macro to micro levels of talk, text, context or society, and vice versa. It may examine ongoing discourse top down, beginning with general abstract patterns, or bottom up, beginning with the nitty-gritty of actually used sounds, words, gestures, meanings or strategies. And perhaps most importantly, *Discourse Analysis* provides the theoretical and methodological tools for a well-founded critical approach to the study of social problems, power and inequality.' (Van Dijk 1997c: 32)

Basic Literature on *Discourse Analysis*

Gee (1999, 2010) presents an intelligible guide to Discourse Analysis that links linguistic and sociological perspectives. Philipps and Hardy (2002), similarly, provide first and foremost an outline of research practice. The manuals edited by Teun van Dijk (1985; 1997a, b) introduce us to linguistic sciences and cognitive psychology; van Dijk (2008a, b) develops a comprehensive theory of the referencing of contexts on the basis of DA. Helpful more recent collections of the approaches collected under the umbrella of DA are provided in Wetherell, Taylor and Yates (2001b), Schiffrin, Tannen and Hamilton (2001) and Cameron (2001). Billig (1996) develops an influential perspective on the relationship between argumentation processes and types of cognition. Wetherell, Taylor and Yates (2001a) and Jaworski and Coupland (2006) present classic basic texts, with orientation to social sciences. Parker and The Bolton Discourse Network explain, in addition, semiotic routes to the analysis of visual documents and further procedures. Gee (1999, 2010) links DA with thoughts on theories of cognitive schemata and with discourse theory. Schiffrin (1994), Ehlich (1994), Fritz and Hundsnurscher (1994) or Brown and Yule (1983) concentrate on linguistic approaches to DA. References to ethnomethodological conversation analysis and sociological linguistic research may be found in Luckmann (1979), McHoul (1994), Eberle (1997), Knoblauch (2000) and Wood and Kroger (2000). Under the heading of Discursive Psychology a new research perspective has developed that investigates psychological questions using the methods of DA (Potter 1996, 2007; Potter and Wetherell 1987; Edwards 1997; Edwards and Potter 1992; Parker 1992).

Van Dijk understands *discourse studies* as interdisciplinary, and in particular as forming a bridge between linguistic and cognitive research. Depending on the question and the (inter)disciplinary perspective between linguistics, cognitive science, psychology and sociology, further specifications of the levels of discourse are necessary. Despite the broad definition of the term 'context', in relation to discourse studies we find predominantly linguistic, conversation and genre-analytical traditions of the analysis of concrete instances of language use in a situational context. Here research interests are directed at formal production rules and genre structures in texts and utterances in a variety of contexts, for example the structure of news items in printed media, at social factors in conversational behaviour, or at basic patterns of oral communicative processes (such as those between teachers and pupils, men and women), at the organization of speaker change, and so on. In this respect, the Discourse Analysis approach *Functional Pragmatics*, for instance, gives the following definition:

> 'Under *discourse* we understand units and forms of speech, or interaction, which may be part of everyday linguistic action, but which may also occur in an institutional setting. (...) From a systematic point of view the co-presence of speaker and listener belong to discourse ("face-to-face interaction"); but this may also be reduced, for example, to temporal co-presence (on the telephone). At the same time the totality of interactions between members of particular social groups (e.g. doctor – patient, scientists, politicians – citizens) or within a designated social area (e.g. teacher-learning-discourse in schools and other educational institutions) may also be summed up as discourse. The concrete forms and sequences of discourses are the subject of *Discourse Analysis*.' (Brünner and Graefen 1994: 7f. Emphasis in original)

Within DA, depending on discipline, question, and research paradigm, there are different and partially irreconcilable perspectives on the object of analysis of a linguistic interaction. From the viewpoint of Functional Pragmatics, for example, the essential difference between Discourse Analysis and conversation analysis lies in the fact that the latter proceeds from the belief that 'given social circumstances are produced by the interactants in conversations' and investigates the '*how*' of such constitutive processes in interaction; Discourse Analysis stresses 'in contrast, the fact that linguistic action is preformed by virtue of social purposes and institutional conditions, and aims at reconstructing the "*why*", the purposive nature of actions' (Brünner and Graefen 1994: 13). On the other hand the kind of Discursive Psychology developed by Jonathan Potter and others, for example, comes close to ethnomethodologically motivated Conversation Analysis; in many survey treatments or introductions into Discourse Analysis the latter is, of course, also included. Variants of conversational research have grown in practical significance as examples of 'Applied Discourse Research'. In these, what is at issue is the development of communicative competences, whether it be in oral or written representation, in conducting a conversation, and joining in discussions through communication training.[10] Although there is also an increasing amount of discussion of links between DA and approaches inspired by discourse theory, so far these different traditions have rarely been taken together in practical research.[11]

Arnulf Deppermann (2008: 9), citing Kallmeyer (1985), distinguishes 6 levels in the constitution of interaction in conversations, which become the object of an analysis of talk as a kind of conversation analysis that is partially extended with categories of an interpretative procedure:

- the investigation of conversational organization (for example, with regard to power processes);
- the analysis of the representation of factual matters (knowledge, classification);
- conversation as goal-directed action;
- social relations between, and identities of the participants;
- the mode of the conversation; and
- the processes of understanding and co-operation (production of reciprocity).

2.3. Discourse Linguistics and (Corpus-based) Linguistic-Historical Analyses of Discourse

In the links between the historical sciences and linguistic research, concepts were developed in the History of Concepts ('Begriffsgeschichte') , Historical Semantics and Discourse History, the roots of which are to be found in the

---

[10]See, for example, Brünner, Fiehler and Kindt (1999), and also the publications of the *Institut für Internationale Kommunikation* (IIK) (www.iik-duesseldorf.de).

[11]See, for example, Miller and Fox (2004), Wetherell (1998), Jørgensen and Phillips (2002), Gee (1999, 2010).

French History of Mentalities of the *Annales-School* and in various approaches within Linguistics. Within these perspectives the term discourse plays a special role whenever large quantities of text (corpora) are analysed. In recent years there has been a heated discussion, particularly in linguistic research, concerning the relationship between 'language and knowledge' – which is the name of a linguistic network – or the processing of 'knowledge through language' (Felder and Müller 2008; Viehöver, Keller and Schneider 2012).[12] In addition, there has been an 'explosive' development of approaches beyond Corpus Linguistics, which have in part brought linguistic research very close to social science research and which have now come to establish an independent area of 'Discourse Linguistics' (e.g. Konerding 2009, Warnke 2007, Warnke and Spitzmüller 2008, Warnke and Spitzmüller 2011, Teubert 2010a,b). According to Konerding (2009: 170ff) present-day developments still seem to be 'rather compilatory and aggregative', and for the next few years more systematic theoretical work will be needed in this area to avoid falling back behind the positions achieved by the first generation of linguistic discourse research (for example, Busse 1987, Busse and Teubert 1994).

Basic Literature on historical, linguistic-historical and linguistic discourse research

Landwehr (2008) gives an introduction to discourse-historical approaches and the perspective of the 'history of what can be said'. Discipline-specific surveys for the historical sciences are to be found in Sarasin (1996, 2003, 2011) and Eder (2006). Landwehr (2010) provides a collection of history and social science analyses on the question of discursive change. The Cambridge School of politico-historical discourse research around Quentin Skinner (1978) and John Pocock (1962, 1965) is presented in Hampsher-Monk (1984) and Tully (1988a,b). The interface between history and linguistics is a main focus in Bödeker (2002), Busse (1987), Maas (1988), Steinmetz (1993) or Busse, Hermanns and Teubert (1994) and, concerning the 'history of concepts', Hampsher-Monk, Tilmans and van Vree (1998). Williams (1999), Charaudeau and Maingueneau (2002) and Guilhaumou (2006, 2010) document the development and status of French historical and

(Continued)

---

[12]Felder and Müller (2008) represent the network 'Language and Knowledge', which is based in Heidelberg.

(Continued)

linguistic discussions of the term discourse, which link, in a very specific fashion, Marxist approaches and Michel Foucault's discourse theory, corpus linguistic and also ethnomethodological approaches. Maingueneau (1976, 1991, 1994, 1995, 2012) explains linguistic approaches to Discourse Analysis in France and focuses on the microanalytic concept of 'utterance analysis', which asks very specifically how speakers are evoked in and through texts. Angermüller (2007) explains this approach and offers examples of actual analyses. Widdowson (2007) provides a concise introduction into questions and concepts in discourse linguistics. Survey treatments with a larger reference to the German approaches to a corpus-oriented history of discourse and developments in linguistics are to be found in Jung (2011), Niehr and Böke (2010), Wengeler (2003), Busse, Niehr and Wengeler (2005) and the papers in Jung, Böke and Wengeler (1997), which present different modes of approach to the analysis of migration discourses. On corpus-based discourse analyses, see also Teubert (1999, 2010a,b) and the publications of the Institute for German Language in Mannheim. In association with the network 'Language and Knowledge' an independent and distinctive 'discourse linguistics' has now been established, whose spectrum of orientations includes Foucault's ideas, discourse hermeneutics (Hermanns 2007), cognition-oriented frame approaches (Busse 2008, Ziem 2008, Konerding 2009: 171ff, Gee 1999) and more markedly social-science-oriented questions (Felder 2009, Felder and Müller 2008, Warnke 2007, Warnke and Spitzmüller 2011). Linguistics has become increasingly interested in questions of multimodality, that is, the interrelation between different sign formats (particularly text and picture) in utterance practices (Kress and van Leeuwen 2001, Bateman 2008, Meier 2008, 2011, Stöckl 2004, Diekmannshenke, Klemm and Stöckl 2010). For a critical discussion of discourse linguistics, see Diaz-Bone (2010).

In corpus linguistics we are concerned with a linguistic approach that brings together comprehensive corpora of data from a large number of individual texts (for example, newspaper articles) according to lexical or thematic (content-based) criteria. Such a corpus is treated as a representative sample, statistically and in terms of content, taken from the virtual total corpus of all the texts that belong to it (the 'discourse') in terms of the selection criterion; from an historical viewpoint this may be arranged synchronically or diachronically, and may contain contemporary or historical texts. Within the corpus a search is made, using statistically-quantitative methods, for connections and distributions of lexical and utterance forms and their changes at given points in time or over a period of time (i.e. synchronically or diachronically).In this process linguistic questions of language change are extended with semantic questions (see the following text box).

The Linguistic Discourse Semantics Approach according to Busse and Teubert (1994:14)

'Under discourses, in terms of research practice, we understand virtual text corpora, the composition of which is governed, in the broadest sense, by content (or semantic) criteria. A discourse includes all the texts which:

- are concerned with a chosen subject, theme, complex of knowledge or concept as their research object, which show mutual semantic relationships and/or which are in a common utterance, communicative, functional, or purposive context;
- fulfil the conditions prescribed in the research programme with regard to temporal extension or period samplings, place, social domains, communicative area, text typology and other parameters; and
- which are related to one another by virtue of explicit or implicit references, or display an intertextual connection

Concrete text corpora (i.e. those underlying a discourse-analytical investigation) are subsets of the discourses in question. In making selections practical considerations such as the availability of sources and relevance criteria based on content, are of primary importance; what is crucial is the researchers' design focus, which constitutes the concrete textual corpus and therefore the object of the investigation. As an example we might cite the 'historians' dispute' ("Historikerstreit"). All the contributions to this debate combined to form the discourse. A concrete corpus for the historians' dispute contains a selection of texts, which, explicitly or implicitly takes a position on this. (…) The history of concepts and discourse should make a contribution to social and cultural history. Language history thus becomes an important element in a social history of linguistically mediated and organized knowledge.'

Prominent forms of corpus-based and historically-oriented Discourse Analysis have been developed since the end of the 1960s, particularly in France, by Michel Pêcheux, Régine Robin, Jacques Guilhaumou, Denise Maldidier and others. This Marxist French school of Discourse Analysis, aiming at the critique of ideology, ties up with the theoretical conceptions and notion of ideology as established by Louis Althusser (2001 [1970]) and also with some of the ideas of Michel Foucault (on this see Chapter 2.4 and 2.6; Guilhaumou 2010, Williams 1999). Language is seen as a materialization of ideologies; the term discourse relates to the ideological side of language use.

Against this theoretical background, strategies of linguistic and quantitative text analysis, following Harris's (1952) Distribution Linguistics, were implemented in order to reconstruct (social) linguistic structures, for example in historical text corpora (such as pamphlets from the time of the French Revolution). For this Pêcheux (1995[1969] and others) developed the project of a computer-supported 'automatic' Discourse Analysis.[13] In the linguistic-historical research that has been, and still is being, carried out by the French school, interest focuses on different levels of analysis: the lexicological level of terms, conceptual fields and lexical field structures (for example, by the analysis of word frequencies), the analysis of semantic fields (related or associated terms), the investigation of the material basis of communication, and more besides. In the course of its development, the French approach to Discourse Analysis has become increasingly open to other discourse-historical, semantic and ethnomethodological analytical traditions, to the English Discourse History of Quentin Skinner, among others, or the German history of concepts and Historical Semantics that was initiated by Reinhart Koselleck. [14]

In more recent German linguistic discourse research Dietrich Busse, Fritz Hermanns, Wolfgang Teubert, as well as Georg Stötzel and his associates have promoted approaches to a linguistic discourse history. Their attention focuses on the semantically-oriented investigation of language change. For this purpose, Matthias Jung, for example, has proposed a 'cube model' of discourse,

---

[13]Pêcheux (1995, 1988); Helsloot and Hak (2007); also Diaz-Bone (2008: 93ff), Macdonell (1986: 43ff) or Fairclough (1992: 30ff). The mediation undertaken by Pêcheux between Althusser and Foucault has influenced the Critical Discourse Analysis of Norman Fairclough, Jürgen Link or Siegfried Jäger (see Chapter 2.4).

[14]For an overview see Williams (1999), Hampsher-Monk, Tilmans and van Vree (1998), Guilhamou (1989, 2006, 2010), Chareaudeau and Mainguenau (2002), Tully (1988a,b).

which sees discourses as virtual corpora of utterances related to a particular topic, for instance, the discourse on 'Atomic Energy' (Jung 2011). From this kind of virtual corpus Discourse Analysis compiles the actual corpus for investigation according to its particular research interests. In this corpus an analysis is then conducted of the change or constancy over time of the terms used, the use of metaphors and arguments, and language reflexivity (in the sense of self-thematization of language use in the utterances) (see text box).[15]

Example of the Procedure in Linguistic Discourse History

'In the investigation of the discourse on atomic energy, but also in the Düsseldorf project on "Discourse of Migration", as a first step, with the help of the register, the corpora of all relevant parliamentary debates were assembled and made machine-readable. Within these corpora, as a second step, we then sought for evidence in context. This takes place in word-level investigation (refugee vs. asylum seeker), or in the context of particular images ("flood-metaphor in migration discourse"). In doing this some data analysis software may be used by applying a pre-defined list of terms to look for. But analysis, if focused on argumentation topoi, may also proceed through traditional reading and classification; this may equally lead to computer assisted quantification, but this is not a must. In the third step, the evidence for which statistical distributions may be produced should then be interpreted in the context of a sentence, text, or whole discourse. (....)

In relation to the discourse on atomic energy since 1900, for example, it becomes clear how greatly false ideas about the use of nuclear fission energy, as a consequence of the conceptualization employed, going back to the beginning of the century, have determined public discourse. In the same way, we can see how the process of changing values appears on the linguistic horizon, to what extent the relative success of the anti-nuclear movement is associated with a new quality in its vocabulary and is part of a general process of emancipation of the lay public, or how much its protagonists have developed a sophisticated new language awareness.' (Jung 2011: 43ff)

---

[15]See Busse, Hermanns and Teubert (1994), Hermanns (1994, 1995), Niehr and Böke (2000, 2010), Wengeler (2003).

The discourse linguistics that are expanding so much in the present day contain a broader spectrum of initial assumptions, research interests and methodological strategies. For instance, questions about the relation between texts and contexts, about the multimodality of the use of signs and about the connection between language and knowledge are now of central importance. Part of the 'foundations and procedures of a type of linguistics beyond textual boundaries' (Warnke and Spitzmüller 2008a), in addition to corpus linguistics, consists of hermeneutic and knowledge-analysis perspectives, together with frame semantics from cognitive science or approaches from social semiotics (Warnke and Spitzmüller 2011, van Leeuwen 2005).[16]

2.4. Critical Discourse Analysis and *Kritische Diskursanalyse*

Under the label Critical Discourse Analysis (CDA) many authors, from various linguistic Discourse Analysis contexts, are working on connections between linguistics and critical analyses of language use, ideologies, and social (de)formations as well as with social science perspectives in more general terms. In this, the goal of an emancipatory explanation, by means of a critique of current practice and related recommendations for improvement, is of equal value to scientific interests. Important exponents of CDA are the Dutch linguist Teun van Dijk, whom we mentioned previously, the Austrian linguist Ruth Wodak and the British researcher Norman Fairclough.[17] If one discounts van Dijk's attempts to relate Discourse Analysis to approaches within cognitive research, the main difference between Discourse Analysis and Critical Discourse Analysis (or *Kritische Diskursanalyse*) lies in the fact that the latter approaches are less concerned with a cognitive orientation and more with a social theory basis for discourse analyses, referring to more or less shared, but always social orders of knowledge. In German-speaking areas the linguist Siegfried Jäger, together with his colleagues at the Duisburg Institute for Linguistic and Social Research (DISS), has developed an independent approach to *Kritische Diskursanalyse*.

---

[16]On this see also the journal *Social Semiotics*.

[17]They all have their own emphases in this. See also the online periodical 'Critical Approaches to Discourse Analysis across Disciplines (CADAAD)', www.cadaad.org/journal.

Text box: Basic Literature on Critical Discourse Analysis and *Kritische Diskursanalyse*

The development and basis of CDA are presented above all in the publications of Fairclough (1989, 1992, 1995, 1998, 2003) and with more recent links to sociological theories or social diagnoses in Chouliaraki and Fairclough (1999). Positions that differ to a greater or lesser extent within CDA are documented in publications by van Dijk (1993), Wodak (1996), Wodak and Meyer (2002), Wodak and Ludwig (1999), Weiss and Wodak (2003) and the comprehensive collection of major texts in Toolan (2002). Jørgensen and Philipps (2002: 60ff), Titscher, Wodak, Meyer and Vetter (2000: 144) and Fairclough and Wodak (1997) provide concise overviews of the basic positions. Billig and Schegloff (1999) discuss the relationship of CDA and Conversation Analysis. The papers in Wodak and Chilton (2005) introduce new perspectives in CDA; van Leeuwen (2008) outlines connections to semiotics and the analysis of visual data. Empirical analyses are to be found in *Discourse and Society* and in the online journal *Critical Approaches to Discourse Analysis across Disciplines* (CA-DAAD). A passionate basic critique of CDA is formulated by Widdowson (2004).

Siegfried Jäger has explained the approach of *Kritische Diskursanalyse* in a book of the same name, first in 1993, and then in a revised form in the following years, both in terms of its foundations and also its procedures, using sample analyses (Jäger 2009). Jäger and Zimmermann (2010) offer a short introduction and outline, in a lexicon, the working concepts of *Kritische Diskursanalyse*. Shorter presentations may be found in Jäger (1999; 2011); and a large number of sample analyses are in Jäger and Jäger (2007).

Critical Discourse Analysis

Since the 1980s Norman Fairclough, one of the most widely-known exponents of CDA, has presented his approach in a large number of publications. He links Marxist philosophical traditions – above all Louis Althusser's concept of ideology and Antonio Gramsci's notion of hegemony – with Foucault's discourse theory, linguistic questions, traditions of critical linguistics and social science theories, and social diagnoses.[18] For the French Marxist, Louis Althusser (2001 [1970]), ideologies are meaning-systems that put individuals into imagined

---

[18]On the link between Discourse Analysis and ideological critique, see Demirovic (1988), Demirovic and Prigge (1988), van Dijk (1998).

relationships with the real relationships in which they live (Macdonell 1986: 27). As a relatively autonomous social level, that is, not immediately dependent on an economic basis, they make a contribution of their own to the reproduction and transformation of economic relations. In this way Althusser abandons an all too narrow Marxist interpretation of foundation-superstructure relations. Of course, this does not mean that ideologies are free-floating ideational structures. On the contrary, Althusser stresses the tripartite relationship between ideologies and material institutions: firstly ideologies are materialized in institutional practices. Secondly, they form the self-image of subjects – they constitute persons and social subjects through processes of positioning (for instance, in the sense of class or ethnicity). And thirdly, this takes place in such different social institutions and organizations as family, law, media, education and more besides. Ideologies are in relationships of competition and hierarchy to one another; the dominant ideology at a particular moment is perceived as the result of class warfare (Fairclough 1992: 30 and 86ff).

Long before Althusser, Antonio Gramsci (2010/2011 [1929–1937] had moved the term 'hegemony' to the centre of his reflections. He used it to mean the dominance, power, and opinion leadership of one economic class and their allies over different social areas or indeed the whole of a society. But for him hegemony is not based on a complete notion of supremacy but only on a more or less partial and time-limited one. This is the result of temporary power alliances which include even the suppressed classes. Hegemony therefore refers to an ultimately precariously and only temporarily stable state in an area of constant struggles for the hegemonic position (Fairclough 1992: 91ff).

The concepts of Althusser, Gramsci and others provide, within CDA, a theoretical background for assumptions about the manner in which social structures determine concrete language events.[19] The definition of discourse formulated by Norman Fairclough and Ruth Wodak (see text box below) and their analytical ideas have many links with Discourse Analysis (see Chapter 2.2); but they differ from this in their foundations in social theory as well as in linguistic theory, and in their explicit social-critical intention. Discourses are defined as language use in speaking and writing *and* simultaneously as one form of social practice (alongside others):

'Describing discourse as social practice implies a dialectical relationship between a particular discursive event and the situation(s), institution(s)

---

[19]Gramsci also influenced the discourse theory of Mouffe and Laclau; see Chapter 2.6.

and social structure(s) which frame it. A dialectical relationship is a two-way relationship: the discursive event is shaped by situations, institutions and social structures, but it also shapes them'. (Fairclough and Wodak 1997: 258)

Language use is, simultaneously, action and processing (including attribution) of sense or meaning; both dimensions can be understood as a social and at the same time socially-structured process. In this a dialectical relationship arises between discourses and the social structures which provide their context: both function reciprocally as conditions and effects. Discourses constitute the world and conversely they are constituted by it; they (re)produce and transform society; they achieve the construction of social identities, the production of social relationships between individuals and the construction of systems of knowledge and belief: 'Discourse is a practice not just of representing the world, but of signifying the world, constituting and constructing the world in meaning' (Fairclough 1992: 64). Discourses are constituted in 'orders of discourse', that is, in sets of conventions for language use that are connected with social institutions.

The *CDA* Approach of Norman Fairclough and Ruth Wodak

'CDA conceptualizes language as a form of social practice, and attempts to make human beings aware of the reciprocal influences of language and social structure of which they are normally unaware (…) CDA sees itself as politically involved research with an emancipatory requirement: it seeks to have an effect on social practice and social relationships, for example in teacher development, in the elaboration of guidelines for non-sexist language use or in proposals to increase the intelligibility of news and legal texts. The research emphases which have arisen in pursuit of these goals include language usage in organizations, and the investigation of prejudice in general, and racism, anti-Semitism and sexism in particular.' (Titscher, Wodak, Meyer and Vetter 2000: 147)

The general principles of CDA may be summarized as follows:

1   CDA is concerned with social problems. It is not concerned with language or language use per se, but with the linguistic character of social and cultural processes and structures. Accordingly, CDA is essentially interdisciplinary

(Continued)

(Continued)

2 Power-relations have to do with discourse (Foucault 2010 [1969/1971], Bourdieu 1984), and CDA studies both power in discourse and power over discourse

3 Society and culture are dialectically related to discourse: society and culture are shaped by discourse, and at the same time constitute discourse. Every single instance of language use reproduces or transforms society and culture, including power relations

4 Language use may be ideological. To determine this it is necessary to analyse texts to investigate their interpretation, reception and social effects

5 Discourses are historical and can only be understood in relation to their context. At the meta-theoretical level this corresponds to the approach of Wittgenstein (1984, § 7), according to which the meaning of an utterance rests in its usage in a particular situation. Discourses are not only embedded in a particular culture, ideology or history, but are also connected intertextually to other discourses

6 The connection between text and society is not direct, but is manifest through some (socio-cognitive) intermediary such as the one advanced in the socio-psychological model of text comprehension (Wodak 1986)

7 Discourse Analysis is interpretative and explanatory. Critical analysis implies a systematic methodology and a relationship between the text and its social conditions, ideologies and power-relations. Interpretations are always dynamic and open to new contexts and new information

8 Discourse is a form of social behaviour. CDA is understood as a social scientific discipline which makes its interests explicit and prefers to apply its discoveries to practical questions. (Titscher, Wodak, Meyer and Vetter 2000: 146, after Wodak 1996: 17–20)

Fairclough distinguishes the following stages in the concrete analysis of discourses: at the centre there is the text, that is, the written or spoken language, the pictures and sounds, produced in a discursive event. Such texts constitute the raw data for CDA. They are analysed, with regard to their production and reception process and its embedding in a context, their form, meaning, strategic language use, vocabulary and so on.[20] Every text is embedded in an instance of discursive practice of text production, dissemination and consumption, and this in turn is embedded in a social practice, a relationship of situational, institutional and social context, for the analysis of which the concepts of

---

[20]Sample applications may be found in the publications already mentioned by Fairclough and Wodak, and also in the journal *Discourse and Society*.

ideology and hegemony are important. Discourses count as ideological to the extent to which (in respect of the critical standards of the discourse analysts) they reinforce established social relationships of power and dominance. The social conditions of text-production and interpretation may be analysed with regard to the levels of the immediate situation, the broader social institutions, and the whole-society context (Fairclough 1992: 225ff).[21] Together with Lili Chouliaraki, Fairclough has extended his approach in recent years, with reference to social science theories and sociological diagnoses of the current situation[22], in pursuit of a kind of social research that is interested in the role, functioning and problems of language as social practice in processes of social change; in this the critical-explanatory intention of producing and disseminating a 'critical discourse awareness' comes into the foreground (Chouliaraki and Fairclough 1999; Fairclough 2011). In accordance with this the methodological proposals are also modified (see text box). Fairclough (2003) concentrates on linguistic questions and methods.

Guidelines for the Procedure of *Critical Discourse Analysis*

Norman Fairclough (1989, 1992) suggests the following steps in an analysis:

1 Definition of the research problem
2 Compilation of the data corpus
3 Completion of the data corpus with supplementary materials

(Continued)

---

[21]Both Wodak and Fairclough favour different methodological procedures depending on the research question; but for both of them the point of departure in linguistic approaches to *Discourse Analysis* remains significant (see Chapter 2.2). Wodak relies in her work on a plurality of methods with backgrounds in cognitive, social-psychological, socio-, psycho- or text linguistics (see, for example, Wodak 1986, 1996, 1997; Wodak et al. 1990: 32ff; Wodak, de Cillia and Reisigl 1998; Titscher, Wodak, Meyer and Vetter 2000: 154ff; Wodak and Chilton 2005). In her investigation of 'Disorders of Discourse' in organizational contexts she uses Habermas's model of discourse ethics (see Chapter 2.1) as a normative parameter for the assessment of the 'distortion' of conversational processes.

[22]For example, Basil Bernstein, Pierre Bourdieu, Michel Foucault, Anthony Giddens, David Harvey, Jürgen Habermas, the Post-modernist debate, Chantal Mouffe and Ernesto Laclau.

(Continued)

4 Transcription of the recorded linguistic data (where necessary)
5 Selection of samples from the corpus
6 Steps in the analysis, consisting of:

- text analysis (topics, structures, vocabulary, grammar, and others)
- analysis of the immediate situational textual context: interpretation of the relationship between text and interactive context; analysis of the social practice to which a discourse belongs (situating it in more general orders of discourse, ideological elements; how do participants interpret the situation? What formal discourse genres and content schemata are employed? Do the discourse participants agree on this, and if not, where do they differ?
- explanation of the relationship between interactive context and social context/macro-analysis of discourse practices. (What power relations influence the situation at the situational, institutional and social levels? What elements of participants' resources are ideological in nature? How is this discourse positioned in respect of power struggles at the situational, institutional and social levels?)

Chouliaraki and Fairclough (1999: 53ff) provide a modified investigative framework:

1 Defining the research problem (addressing a concrete, observable problematic relation between discourse and social practice: the linked activities and their interpretation)
2 Identifying obstacles to be tackled:

i analysis of the conjuncture of practices to which the discourse under analysis belongs;
ii analysis of the relevant practice identified as problematic;
iii analysis of the more general discourse, its structures and interactive production

3 Analysing the problem's function in the practice concerned
4 Exploring possible ways to change or exclude the obstacles
5 Reflection on the researcher's position towards the problem and the analytical procedure

---

Kritische Diskursanalyse

In German-speaking areas of the world the linguist Siegfried Jäger and his colleagues at the Duisburg Institute for Linguistic and Social Research (DISS) have developed a specific approach to *Kritische Diskursanalyse*. This is also primarily linguistic in its basis, but differs from the CDA outlined above in its theoretical foundation. Jäger (2009, 2011; see also Jäger and Zimmermann 2010) builds essentially on the work of Michel Foucault, its reception and dissemination by the literary theorist Jürgen Link (1995, 2011), and also the Marxist-psychological activity theory of A.N. Leontiev (1978).

During the 1980s Jürgen Link, together with Ursula Link-Heer and other collaborators, developed an ideologically critical perspective on discourse theory and analysis (Link 2011). This was conducted in the 'kultuRRevolution.zeitschrift für diskurstheorie' (cultural revolution. Journal for discourse theory), while the author was discussing the French analyse du discours (see Chapter 2.3). In essence this concerns the investigation of inter-discursive relationships between different discourses, and in particular with the functioning of social collective symbols (see text box).[23]

The discourse-theoretical approach of Jürgen Link[24]

Jürgen Link adopts concepts from Michel Foucault and the Marxist linguist Michel Pêcheux. Following Foucault he sees Diskurs (discourse) as 'an institutionalized specialist knowledge, including the corresponding ritualized forms of speech, modes of action and power-effects.'

By Inter-diskurs (inter-discourse) Link means:

the totality of all the discourse elements (...) that are not special but are common to a number of individual discourses. As is shown by the example of 'fairness', particular discourse elements migrate as metaphors from a special initial discourse – here that of sport – crossing a number of discourses (for example those of politics, the law, and so on), and as a result they become spontaneously fundamental ideological concepts of civil society. In this it is supremely important that the inter-discourse of civil society is also discourse in Foucault's sense, which means that here, too, ritualized forms of speech, modes of action and power-effects are coupled.

(Continued)

---

[23]Corresponding discourse analyses are to be found in the journal *kultuRRevolution*.

[24]Highlighting as in the original. See the instructive interviews with Jürgen Link and Siegfried Jäger by Diaz-Bone (2006a, b); also the works of Pêcheux (1984, 1995); Link (1982, 1983, 1984, 1988, 1999, 2011); Link and Link-Heer (1990); Parr and Thiele (2010); Demirovic (1988); Jäger (2009).

(Continued)

The 'total area of the symbolism of imagery, metaphor, illustrative stereotypes and clichés' constitutes 'the synchronic system of collective symbols' (SySyKoll)

'I speak of a synchronic system because all the collective symbols of a culture (e.g. *football, car, aeroplane, rockets, cancer* and so on) generate, not individually but always in concert, partial structures of the inter-discourse. A symptom of this is the basic figure of *journalistic inter-discourse*, the so-called "catachresis-meander", according to the model: "*the wave of cuts into the social welfare system has to be stemmed by stimulating the engine of economic growth*".'[25]

The term *discursive position* is suggested for a particular relatively coherent application of the system of collective symbols:

'As an example of this, for us in West Germany we might cite the current example of the ecological movement and the 'Green' Party. Since there have been industrial societies, there has been an inter-discursive position that might be described as "Rousseauistic": in this the industrialist symbols (such as machine, *metropolis* and so on) have been negatively evaluated and set against positively evaluated natural symbols. (…) The opposite discursive position, which is enthusiastic about *concrete, machines and rockets*, has therefore been put totally on the defensive in the space of a few years. This sort of process is of course dependent on real developments (ecological crisis, *forest death*, and so on), as a result of which "discursive events" appear (…); such "discursive events strengthen or weaken one discursive position or another".' (all quotations derived from Link 1988: 48)

Processes of public discussion are seen as elaborations of inter-discursive elements.

Texts, in the sense of Leontiev's activity theory (Leontiev 1978), are the results of the thinking activities of individuals. Their production is based on knowledge acquired in processes of socialization, the particular motives of those engaged in linguistic action and the available resources of verbalization. Discourses are defined by Jäger as 'flows of social stocks of knowledge

---

[25]'Die Welle von Einschnitten ins soziale Netz muß durch die Ankurbelung des Konjunkturmotors eingedeicht werden.'

through time' (Jäger 2009: 158) or, following Link, as 'institutionalized rule-governed modes of speaking, insofar as they are coupled with actions and thus exert power effects' (Jürgen Link, cited in Jäger 2009: 127).

The Procedure of *Kritische Diskursanalyse*

Siegfried Jäger recently proposed the following steps of analysis:

1 Presentation and justification of the topic (Discourse thread);
2 Brief characterization (of the sector) of the discourse level;
3 Identification of the discursive context and the relevant discursive events;
4 Obtaining the data corpus/development and preparation of the material base or the archive;
5 Structural analysis: evaluation of the collected data material in respect of the discourse thread to be analysed;
6 Detailed analysis of one or more discourse fragments typical of the discourse position (see the more detailed analytical guidelines in Jäger 2010: 104ff):

   – identification of the institutional framework (medium, genre, motivation etc.)
   – analysis of the textual surface (composition, topics and so on)
   – analysis of the linguistic-rhetorical devices employed (micro-analysis)
   – analysis of the textual-ideological statements (conception of humanity, understanding of society, etc.)

7 Interpretation (systematic overall presentation of the analytical steps and the discourse fragment, message, medium, goals, intended effect, discursive context);
8 Overall analysis of the discourse thread;
9 Analysis of the total discourse through synoptic, summarizing-comparative analysis of different discourse threads. (Jäger 2009: 172ff; 2010: 104ff)

Text analysis becomes Discourse Analysis when texts are understood as elements in a supra-individual and socio-historical discourse:

'I characterize these elements as *discourse fragments*. They *are* components or fragments of the *discourse threads* (= sequences of discourse fragments with a common theme), they move at different discourse levels (= locations from which speech originates, such as science, politics, the media, everyday affairs etc.) and in their totality constitute the *overall discourse* of a society, which may be imagined as a large seething mass; at the same time the discourses (that is, this whole discursive turmoil) constitute the particular preconditions for the further course of the whole-society discourse.' (Jäger 2009: 117)

Discourse structures are explored with reference to the terms 'special discourse' or 'interdiscourse', 'discourse thread' and its interweaving, 'discursive event', 'discursive context', 'discourse level', and principal and subordinate 'themes' (Jäger 2009: 158ff). The methodological procedure, according to the first version of *Kritische Diskursanalyse*, was initially oriented more strongly towards linguistic text approaches, but more recently it has placed more emphasis on processes of interpretation. In addition, it has been extended with elements of a 'dispositive analysis', which aims – beyond the textual level – at the analysis of 'concrete' manifestations of discourses. The principal objects of previous investigations were analyses of 'racist' use of language as found in interviews and media texts. These studies reconstructed the collective symbols used in such documents, the meaning fields established, the use of pronouns, the function of proverbs and figures of speech, the appearing narrative structures and so on (Jäger, M. 2010; Jäger 1992; Jäger and Jäger 2007). The aim of investigations of right-wing extremist discourse is to work out:

> 'in what form, with what content it appears and with the aid of what strategies it is expressed "in the basic social sphere of everyday life". (...) Two of the things Discourse Analysis is concerned with are questioning discourses as to their content and strategies, and determining the influence of special discourses on inter-discourse (frequently via the media, education, powerful institutions and organizations) in brief, it is concerned with making them transparent. (...) Discourse Analysis is concerned with linguistic texts (of all kinds) i.e. from the outset in their relationship to their socio-historical background, by which they are fed and which they refer to, or on which, in turn, they have a (greater or lesser) influence.' (Jäger 1992: 12ff)

2.5 Culturalist Discourse Research

By *culturalist* I mean discourse-oriented perspectives which, unlike the previously described linguistic or, in terms of Marxist ideology, critical uses of the term discourse, have developed within traditions of sociological theory (in the narrower sense). This involves a – more or less convenient – collective term for different preoccupations with the social significance of symbolic orders. These include approaches which stem from the tradition of the interpretative paradigm of sociology and which were formulated there within the framework of Symbolic Interactionism (Plummer 1991) – for example by Joseph R. Gusfield, Robert Wuthnow or William Gamson. Such perspectives proceed on the assumption that, in collective processes of interpretation, social actors negotiate definitions of reality and symbolic orders interactively. The latter, as a socially stabilized reservoir of knowledge and meaning, are always, as historical *a priori*, given to the actors and their use of signs.[26] On the other hand I also include here certain proposals of the French sociologist Pierre Bourdieu, who, in spite of his frequent sweeping criticism of the 'subjectivism' of the interpretative paradigm, has incorporated many of the assumptions outlined there into his theory of practice and his analyses of (linguistically mediated) symbolic battles. In this respect his special interest concerns the analysis of the meaning of language and knowledge in the discussion of the legitimacy of symbolic orders, for example in the application of specific classifications in the power struggles of social groups. Although both the approaches and the authors of the interpretative paradigm, as well as Pierre Bourdieu's ideas, have hitherto seemed comparatively marginal in discourse research, they are of particular interest to social science analyses of discourse, since they stress the behaviour of social actors and the significance of public conflicts of definition. By virtue of the prominence they give to the active and interpretative achievements of social actors in the creation, (re)production and transformation of symbolic orders in discourse, the proponents of *Culturalist Discourse Research* again distinguish themselves from the *Discourse Theories* that we shall present in section 2.6 below.[27]

Pierre Bourdieu: Linguistic usage as a Symbolic Struggle

The sociologist Pierre Bourdieu in his 'Theory of Practice' has suggested a number of basic concepts of sociological analysis that are important for a social science approach to discourse research. Apart from his view of human

---

[26]See Plummer (1991), Keller (2009), Berger and Luckmann (1975 [1966]), Geertz (1973), Keller (2005a, 2011a,b). Some elements of this branch of Culturalist Discourse Research have influenced more recent research undertakings in Discourse Analysis that link them to Foucauldian discourse theory (see Chapter 2.7).

[27]Cultural Studies mediates between these approaches.

speaking, these include the concepts of *habitus*, types of capital, social space and life-styles, and social fields (see Grenfell 2008). 'Habitus' he characterizes as an incorporated system of perceptual, cognitive and performative schemata which individuals construct in the process of socialization. The specific and socio-structurally shaped dispositive structure of habitus depends on the social field and the position in social space, that is to say in discoverable institutional conditions, capital structures and symbolic orders, in the context of which the habitus of an individual is formed. Specific compositions of capital availability – covering economic, social and cultural capital – and the means of their deployment are linked to such positions. 'Symbolic capital' frequently denotes the form of other capitals that is publicly recognized as legitimate. The habitus structures the action and linguistic practice of individuals and thus the (re)production of symbolic orders:

> 'Every practice implies cognitive operations, mobilizes mental representations and, thereby, structuring and organizing schemata of what is and what must be done. Social practice, as Bourdieu insists, is a classifying practice, a practice that is ordered and structured through systems of classification. Perception is guided by means of ideas of order which prescribe not only how the world is seen, but also what can be perceived at all to which our attention is directed.' (Krais 1993: 211)

Language use as the practice of speaking and writing is therefore in one respect coloured by the acquired habitus. Every statement is a contribution – a manifestation or a transformation – to a specific symbolic order, within which it acquires its meaning.[28] The social value of statements, however, is always dependent on its institutional location, or its social position within a field from which it is formulated. This position regulates both the possibilities of production and the different forms of reception of statements:

> 'The field keeps speaker-positions ready which can be assumed by people who are authorized by the field. One group may control discourses in the field in which it controls the occupation of such positions. The authority of a speaker, his symbolic capital, is a derived capital, which (...) is produced in the field and is accumulated by an institution or group. Authority is obtained by a particular speaker because he emerges as the legitimate speaker for a group or institution for which he is a delegate. (...) In order for the symbolic capital to function as a potential,

---

[28]Bourdieu (1984: 486) speaks of a 'universe of discourse' (see Chapter 2.1).

i.e. in order that recognition may be given to the legitimate speaker, the discourse must take place in a legitimate speaking situation (it must be addressed in the right place, at the right time, to the right listener) and it must follow the correct form (figures of speech, forms of address, linguistic style and so on).' (Diaz-Bone 2008: 55f)

In his social theory Bourdieu finally stresses the significance of social struggles concerning the implementation of legitimate symbolic orders or representations of reality. The social classes, in the framework of the different social fields, are entangled in classification struggles. The power of legitimate naming and interpretation of the world's 'real' reality is not entirely, but nonetheless essentially, concentrated in the state and its organs, but is constantly challenged by collective social actors. Cultural disagreements, such as those concerning 'legitimate taste', are classification struggles of different social groups. In this process every piece of linguistic usage is a contribution in the struggle for interpretative power, a stabilization or questioning of relationships of symbolic dominance (Bourdieu 1984, 1990a,b, 1992).[29] As an example Pierre Bourdieu and Luc Boltanski showed this in an (experimentally enhanced) text that first appeared in 1976 and was recently reissued, for the 'Production of Dominant Ideology'. In this classic work of (ideologically) critical Discourse Analysis, Bourdieu and Boltanski present an encyclopaedia of 'dominant principles' composed of citations and analyze, for example, the meaning-structuring differences between 'earlier times' and 'today', the role of evolutionary assumptions, and more besides. Apart from this early and explicit concern with a type of discourse, in Bourdieu's other 'scattered' treatments of the relationship between linguistic practice and symbolic orders no particular value is attached to the term discourse. They may, however, be invoked as a basis of approaches in Discourse Analysis and discourse theory, on the one hand because they examine the occasional neglect, found in Discourse Analysis, of the social circumstances of the communicative situation. On the other hand, such a Bourdieusian perspective confronts certain approaches to discourse theory, which (only) focus on semantic-symbolic structuring, with the challenge that they should investigate concrete discourse

---

[29]Bourdieu has been repeatedly concerned with processes of classification (in schools, universities, at the level of judgements of taste, and more besides), but, with the exception of Bourdieu and Boltanski (2008), he has never presented any systematic analyses of the structures and sequencing of discourses. His references to the dominance and ordering functions of language are predominantly formulated as theoretical proposals.

practices and their institutional embedding in order to fully account for discourse phenomena.[30] For this more recent examples are to be found in the historical sciences (see text box)

Roger Chartier: Perspectives of an historical Discourse Analysis, based on Emile Durkheim, Marcel Mauss, Michel Foucault and Pierre Bourdieu

'This book (...) will, in the first place, demonstrate how – at different times and in different places – an historical reality became tangible, thinkable, legible. This can only be done in a number of steps. Firstly we are concerned with the classifications, divisions and separations that underlie our knowledge of the social world as categorical forms of the observation and assessment of reality. They are based on the fixed and independent predispositions of the group in question, and they vary according to social level or intellectual environment. These inbuilt intellectual schemata produce those configurations by virtue of which the present can acquire meaning, the *alter* may become intelligible and space recognizable. (...) And so in every case it means relating talk to the attitude of the one who is talking. (...) My work aims at the manner in which elites (of very different types – churchmen, public servants, enlightened "notables", social scientists) understood and revealed a portion of reality in which they lived. (...) The representations that we are talking of here are always in competitive situations in which it is a question of power and domination. The struggles in the area of these representations are no less important than economic battles, if one wishes to understand the mechanisms by means of which one group imposes or seeks to impose its view of the social world, its values and its domination. Those who are concerned with conflicts of classification and selection do not distance themselves, as a shortsighted view of

---

[30]In this respect Bourdieu's approach complements Foucault's discourse theory. Rainer Diaz-Bone (2008), in his 'discourse theoretical extension of Bourdieu's distinction theory', is aiming at striking a balance between the approaches of Bourdieu and Foucault. Using the examples of the musical genres 'Heavy metal' and 'Techno', he shows that Bourdieu's theory of 'fine distinctions' requires supplementation in discourse theory, since it will otherwise be unclear from where individuals are invoking the classifications, knowledge, and evaluative schemata that they use in linguistic and behavioural practice. In the context of the critique of Bourdieu, which has meanwhile appeared very powerful in France, accusing him of a very restricted understanding of social mechanisms, former disciples of Bourdieu, such as Bernard Lahire, are suggesting the use of Foucault's theoretical concepts to enlarge horizons, rather than Bourdieu's 'reductionism'.

history maintained for many years, from the social dimension, but are able, conversely, to set up combat zones which are the more decisive, the less materially tangible they are.' (Chartier 1992: 11f; see also Chartier 1989)

William A. Gamson: Frame-Analysis of Public Discourse

As a representative of the interpretative paradigm William A. Gamson and his associates made suggestions in the 1980s for the analysis of processes of public discussion – for example about affirmative action (Gamson and Modigliani 1987) or nuclear energy (Gamson and Modigliani 1989) – as discourses.[31] What is specific to this approach is the linking of qualitative text analyses with a quantifying analysis of large corpora of data taken from articles in the print media. Pictorial representations (such as cartoons) are also investigated. Gamson developed *frame analysis* – as he calls his approach, following Erving Goffman (1974) – in the context of symbolic-interactionist research into the processes of mobilization in social movements. Movements of this sort are bound up with theme-specific interpretative battles about the appropriate interpretation of socio-political problems. In movement research, a link was made in the mid-1980s with Goffman's term 'frame analysis', to investigate processes of the mobilization of agreement through the use of specific interpretative strategies. Movement actors (and others), in public discussions of difficult issues, construct their interpretations of problems with the strategic intention of achieving the largest possible public resonance, and presenting themselves as legitimate and responsible actors and providers of solutions to problems (Gerhards 1992). For example, a reference to the risk of nuclear power stations becoming military targets in the event of war may serve to create a bond between the anti-nuclear and peace movements. Gamson views public debates that are documented in the print media as manifestations of the interpretative conflicts mentioned above. In this sense the media may be seen as a central area for the social construction of reality.

Gamson's suggestion is aimed at the mass analysis of extensive quantities of data. For this, two methodological steps are necessary: first, there is a

---

[31]The concept of 'frame' oscillates between an interpretative paradigm and cognitive anthropology. See Gamson and Lasch 1983, Gamson (1988a), Gamson et al. (1992), Gamson and Stuart (1992), Donati (2011) as an extended discussion; Gee (1999) and Ziem (2008) on a more recent cognition-oriented reception in linguistics. Whether, as frequently postulated, Goffman's concept of frame is compatible with that of cognitive anthropology is a matter of doubt.

qualitative microanalysis of individual texts or pictures. These are understood as components of a discourse that is identifiable according to thematic criteria, and in the first interpretative process they are analyzed with regard to their most important meaning-bearing constituents. The most important components of the meaning of a discourse – such as metaphors or 'catch phrases' – are bundled into meaning 'packages'. Such packages have a specific internal structure. The point of departure is therefore that every package always has at its core a central meaning pattern or 'frame' – for example an idea of 'nature' as a 'complex clock like mechanism' (Donati 2011: 159) – 'The frame suggests what the issue is about' (Gamson 1988b: 165). Then a distinction can be made between 'reasoning devices' and 'framing devices', (for example, metaphors or condensing symbols), which are used for the linguistic-symbolic materialization of the frame. Finally, 'packages' are given a 'storyline' or 'scenario', by means of which they integrate new events over the course of time.

As a second step, after the various typical components of a 'package' have been reconstructed in a qualitative analysis of sample texts, a coding scheme is developed from this for the processing of larger quantities of data. Here the occurrence of specific elements of argument and meaning, in a text that is to be coded, counts as an index for the occurrence of the particular 'package' from which it comes. Discourse positions, therefore, do not always have to be reproduced in full. There is an underlying assumption that the occurrence of specific package-elements in a text (such as an image or a metaphor) elicit the manifestation of the relevant meaning framework and thus of the whole package in the mind of every recipient. Nevertheless nothing is said here about the position of the recipient – for example, agreement or rejection. With the help of the coding schemata developed in this way, large quantities of text may be investigated in respect of the occurrence of the reconstructed 'packages'. The approach of Gamson and others is particularly suited to the analysis of the progress of topics in the mass media, and in the 1990s it inspired discourse-oriented research in Germany, or investigations of political debates on environmental matters, processes of mobilization in social movements, or public controversy concerning abortion, and many more besides; in connection with this, specific modifications and further developments were undertaken.[32]

---

[32]On waste issues see Keller (1998); on climate change Viehöver (2010); on Chernobyl media-reporting Poferl (1997); on social movements, processes of mobilization Gerhards (1992), on public debates on abortion Ferree, Gamson, Gerhards and Rucht (2002), and on the genome debate Gerhards and Schäfer (2006).

In their study of public discourse on atomic energy Gamson and Modigliani (1989) first reconstruct the different mutually competing partial discourses, with the aim of producing a grid of the symbolic and rhetorical means that are employed. This grid serves to determine the representation in the media of these typified discourses in the context of a broad sample from (print) media texts over the past 30 years. There is also an investigation of what representations and interpretations of the topic 'atomic energy' (such as 'playing with fire' or as a 'guarantee of progress') occur in the newspaper texts and with what frequency. Further research interests look at how and why particular carrier groups – so-called 'sponsors' – support discourses, and what traces are left in everyday life by discourses transmitted via the media.

Joseph R. Gusfield: The Culture of Public Problems

Since about the middle of the 1960s, representatives of Symbolic Interactionism such as Howard Becker or Joseph Gusfield have been concerned with the collective public definition of social problems and deviant behaviour. In his analyses of the social construction of public representations of alcohol problems that are primarily devoted to the role of science and law and the relationship between public discourses and individual modes of behaviour, Gusfield has developed a conceptual approach containing many elements of a discourse analytical perspective (Gusfield 1981, 1996). Using ethnographic and text-interpretative methods, he builds on the works of Berger and Luckmann (1975 [1966]) and Kenneth Burke (e.g. Burke 1945).[33] Gusfield investigates the course of controversial public definitions of problems in respect of their concrete material aspects (what institutions, with what methods and consequences), at their semantic-symbolic level, the various actors caught up in conflicts, and the linguistic, argumentation and visualization strategies that are used. In this he emphasizes the power to constitute reality established by the symbolic orders produced and their function in excluding other interpretations. Public discourses are

---

[33]Burke developed important elements of a theory of the human use of symbols in action and language; he emphasizes the meaning of symbolic orders for individuals' definitions of the situation. Gusfield (1989) discusses the relationships of the work of Burke to Charles W. Mills, Erving Goffmann, Alfred Schütz, Michel Foucault, Antonio Gramsci and others.

considered as areas of reality *sui generis*. Their social function is located in ritualistically recalling and performing the fundamental possibility for the existence of symbolic and thereby also social order. [34] A good illustration of this perspective can be found in his investigation of the public discourse on 'drunken driving'. This deals with the manner in which a social phenomenon – driving under the influence of alcohol – becomes a public problem and in the process undergoes a specific interpretation, to which particular institutional and material consequences are attached. Without the term 'discourse' actually appearing – Gusfield speaks of the 'culture of public problems' – essential aspects of a discourse-analytical perspective become clear (see text box).

Joseph Gusfield: 'The culture of public problems: drinking driving and the moral order'

'In analyzing the public character of a problem it is vital to recognize again the multiple possibilities of resolution. Who and what institution gains or is given the responsibility for "doing something" about the issue? As phenomena are open to various modes of conceptualizing them as problems, so too their public character is open to various means of conceiving their resolution. (...) The problem of responsibility has both a cultural and a structural dimension. At the cultural level it implies a way of seeing phenomena. Fixing responsibility for preventing accidents by laws against drinking-driving involves seeing drinking-driving as a choice by a wilful person. Seeing it as a medical problem involves an attribution of compulsion and illness. At a structural level, however, fixing responsibility implies different institutions and different personnel who are charged with obligations and opportunities to attack the problem. Here, too, change from one set of causal definitions, of cognitive conceptualizations, to another carries implications for institutions. (...) Analyzing public problems as structured means finding the conceptual and institutional orderliness in which they emerge in the public arena. The public arena is not a field on which all can play on equal terms; some have greater access than others and greater power

---

[34]As far as I know Gusfield never developed his approach into a systematic procedure for discourse research.

and ability to shape the definition of public issues. (...) The social construction of public problems implies a historical dimension. The same
"objective" condition may be defined as a problem in one time period,
not in another. (...) Structure is process frozen in time as orderliness. It
is a conceptual tool with which to try to make that process understandable. What is important to my thought here is that all is not situational;
ideas and events are contained in an imprecise and changing container.'
(Gusfield 1981: 5ff)

Robert Wuthnow: The Analysis of Communities of Discourse

Robert Wuthnow (1989) employs the term discourse in his investigation of
the relationship between ideas or ideologies and social change, using the
examples of the rise of Protestantism, the Enlightenment or the development of European socialism in the nineteenth century. In this he develops
a conceptual grid, with which it is possible to analyse how social groups
become the carriers of particular ideas, how they articulate and dissemi-
nate them, which ideas are successful (i.e. capable of resonance) in this
process, how they are institutionalized, and what social consequences this
has. As a concept the term discourse is used here in a rather everyday
linguistic form. It designates the linguistic actions and positions of social
actors (for example, the discourse of the Reformers), who in turn form
discourse communities:

'Discourse subsumes the written as well as the verbal, the formal as well
as the informal, the gestural or ritual as well as the conceptual. It occurs,
however, within communities in the broadest sense of the word: communities of competing producers, of interpreters and critics, of audi-
ences and consumers, and of patrons and other significant actors who
become the subjects of discourse itself. It is only in these concrete living and breathing communities that discourse becomes meaningful.'
(Wuthnow 1989: 16)

Wuthnow distinguishes several levels of focus in a corresponding analysis of discourse: the general contextual conditions of a whole society,
and more situational, organizational or institutional contexts and action
sequences within these concrete contexts. The process of the articulation
of positions may be further differentiated into the dimensions of the production and dissemination of ideas, the selection of specific textual and

linguistic genres, and finally the institutionalization of these elements. The term *discursive field* refers to:

> 'a symbolic space or structure within the ideology itself. In the ideologies to be considered here a relatively simple discursive field defined by some fundamental opposition of binary concepts is often evident, but more complex discursive structures are sometimes evident as well. In Luther's discourse a recurrent theme consists of the opposition between the received authority of the church on the one hand and the authority of the Word of God on the other hand. The received authority of the church was a matter of coercion, of chains and imprisonment (...), part of "Satan's plan". (...) The Word of God, in contrast, offered freedom, liberty. (...) These oppositions define a basic polarity that gives structure and organization to Luther's reforming ideology. Many of his observations about specific social or theological issues are mapped onto this basic discursive field. They give it objectivity; it in turn organizes the relations among them, thereby shaping the manner in which they are interpreted. A discursive field of this kind provides the fundamental categories in which thinking can take place. It establishes the limits of discussion and defines the range of problems that can be addressed'. (Wuthnow 1989: 13)

2.6. Discourse Theories

Under the heading of *Discourse Theories*, we will now consider three discourse perspectives that have developed within, or in response to, French Post-structuralism (see Chapter 2.1). We shall first be concerned with the French philosopher Michel Foucault, whose work has probably made a greater contribution to the popularity of the term discourse than that of any other writer. Following this there will be an explanation of the post-Marxist discourse theory of Chantal Mouffe and Ernesto Laclau that developed in the context of political science. Finally there will be a brief discussion of the significance of the concept of discourse in *Cultural Studies*, *Research in Women's and Gender Studies*, and *Post-colonialism*.

Michel Foucault

The current boom in the concept of discourse is largely a result of the work of Michel Foucault in the 1960s and 1970s. As a philosopher interested in history, Foucault was able, in an influential fashion, to formulate new questions and procedures in subject areas related to historical studies. In this he concerned himself with such phenomena as mental illness, penal procedures, the origin and growth of the academic disciplines of psychology, law or medicine, the development of sexuality-related ethical and moral values, and the genealogy of modern conceptions of 'the subject'– the main idea underlying all his work. In such books as *L'ordre du discours* (*Orders of Discourse*, published in 1971, translated in 1972 as The Discourse on Language and included in Foucault 2010) and *L'archéologie du savoir*, published in 1969 (*The Archaeology of Knowledge*, Foucault 2010) and in many essays (e.g. Foucault 1991a, b) there are basic ideas for his theory and empirical studies of discourses.[35]

The far-reaching influence that emanates from Foucault's work is due not so much – and perhaps not even primarily – to his theoretical and methodological writings as to his impressive material analyses. The latter include his investigation of the history of madness and civilization (Foucault 1988a; French original, 1961), of the medical gaze (in *The Birth of the Clinic;* 1994 [1963]), of the the ways in which societies discipline and punish (Foucault 1977a, [1975]), or the history of sexuality (vols 1, 2 and 3, Foucault 1988-1990 [1976, 1984, 1984]), where he was looking at sexuality and technologies or ethics of self-discipline. Through these he directs the understanding of discourses to the academic disciplines, humanities, psychology, law, medicine, philosophy and religion as the locations or institutions within which discourses arise, where they are rooted and develop. Foucault does not approach his research objects as obviously given ahistorical data. He embraces, rather, a sociology of knowledge and constructivist perspective on them: he regards them as contingent phenomena that owe their existence to different configurations of knowledge and practice. In other words, they are constituted on the one hand in the medium of knowledge and on the other hand as social practices. There is, for example, no ahistorical essential quality of madness, but historically different forms of knowledge and practices for dealing with it which determine such qualities and which change over the course of time. 'Madness' only 'exists' in a historically contingent form.

---

[35]See also the complete edition of his various 'Speeches and Writings' (Foucault 2001, 2002, 2003, 2005). The presentation which follows takes up those aspects of his work that are significant for discourse theory and research.

Writing Foucault – some references

There are many introductions into the work of Michel Foucault. See, for example, Danaher, Schirato and Webb (2000), Dreyfus and Rabinow (1982), Deleuze (1988), Smart (2002), Kendall and Wickham (1999), Bublitz (1999), Eribon (1992), Burchell, Gordon and Miller (1991), Fox (1998), Keller (2008). More recent discussions of Foucault's perspectives may be found in Keller, Hirseland, Schneider and Viehöver (2005, 2010, 2011,2012), Bublitz, Bührmann, Hanke and Seier (1999), Keller (2005a), Eder (2006), Bührmann et al. (2007), and also in the *Introductory Literature* cited above (Chapter 2.1), in the context of *Linguistic and Historical Conceptions of Discourse*, and *Kritische Diskursanalyse*.

Current investigations in the area of 'Governmentality Studies' are also significant (Dean 1999; Bröckling, Krasmann and Lemke 2000; Bröckling 2007; Rose, O'Malley, and Valverde 2009). Foucault's views were and are important for discussions within feminism and for the debate in Post-colonialism (Mills 2004; Hark 2011).

Analyses of discourse that are primarily linked to the work of Foucault have more recently been produced, among others, by Anne Waldschmidt (1996, 2010) on the 'Subject of Human Genetics', Sabine Maasen (1998, 2010) with her 'Genealogy of Immorality', the working group of Hannelore Bublitz (1998, Bublitz, Hanke and Seier 2000), with their investigation into representations of gender in discourses on culture at the end of the 19th/beginning of the twentieth century, the historian Jürgen Martschukat (2000) on the death penalty in the eighteenth and nineteenth centuries or the historian Philipp Sarasin with his 'History of the Body' (Sarasin 2001), by political scientists Maarten Hajer (1995) on 'acid rain' and Herbert Gottweis (1998) on the 'Governing of Molecules'. Social discussions of the environment, with an orientation towards Foucault, also became the subject of discourse analyses (e.g. Darier 1999).

In the various stages of his work Foucault made differently accented proposals for a theory and methodology of historical research that were concerned with the concept of discourse. The first phase was marked by a more structuralist orientation; its principal works may be seen as the 1966 study on the *Les mots et les choses* (The Order of Things, Foucault 1991c) and then the aforementioned *L'Archéologie du savoir* (The Archaeology of Knowledge, Foucault 2010) from the year 1969, where he was concerned retrospectively to develop a conceptual framework for analyses of discourse. A first approach to this perspective was suggested in the work programme that was formulated in *Les mots et les choses*:

'What I wished to do was to present, side by side, a definite number of elements: the knowledge of living beings, the knowledge of the laws of language, and the knowledge of economic facts, and to relate them to the philosophical discourse that was contemporary with them during a period extending from the seventeenth to the nineteenth century. (...) Frontiers are redrawn and things usually far apart are brought closer, and vice versa: instead of relating the biological taxonomies to other knowledge of the living being (the theory of germination, or the physiology of animal movement, or the statics of plants), I have compared them with what might have been said at the same time about linguistic signs, the formation of general ideas, the language of action, the hierarchy of needs, and the exchange of goods.' (Foucault 1991c [1966]: x)

Foucault then asks what basic structure, what 'episteme', underlies the widely different scientific classification processes in specific historical ages. Different eras can then be precisely described in terms of the principles by which they order worldly matters – principles transcending, by and large, the borders of particular disciplines. Here Foucault is proceeding from observable regularities in (particularly scientific) texts to an underlying rule-governed structure, a code. Foucault characterizes his mode of procedure in this phase as 'archaeology': he excavates the orders of knowledge of past ages, without expressing an opinion on their truth and meaning content. He rejects historical procedures which are geared to class interests or the whims of individual subjects (for example, 'scientific geniuses'), or which trace, from a hermeneutic perspective, the intentions of authors of past works.[36] Analytical description should take the place of such approaches to history, arguing in terms of succession in time but not in terms of causally sequential circumstances. In the sense of quantitative or serial history it is a matter of investigating what was 'actually' said, i.e. it is a matter of describing and analyzing the material existence of discourses in the shape of definite speech acts. The term 'discourse' – in Foucault's opinion – characterizes a quantity of dispersed statements which appear in different

---

[36]The oft-quoted criticism of a 'Hermeneutics of Suspicion' – a term from Paul Ricœur, directed towards Marxism and psychoanalysis – is related to the rejection of the wholesale subordination of particular determining factors that are behind statements (for example in the sense of the Marxist *Basis-Überbau* assumption). Of course the description of regularities also depends on processes of meaning and understanding that are only intelligible as hermeneutic interpretation. Kendall and Wickham (1999) stress Foucault's affinity to ethnomethodology. The programme of 'archaeology' is to be understood against the background of 'serial history', i.e. a kind of historical writing that investigates large data corpora – e.g. trade statistics, costs of foodstuffs – for different historical periods and looks for patterns or relationships (Chartier 1989, 1992).

places, which have been formed according to the same pattern or rule-system and which can therefore be attributed to one and the same discourse and constitute its objects. The task of the discourse analyst is then the reconstruction of this rule system; in this way it is possible to account for the fact that statements belong to a discourse which was initially only hypothetical:

> 'Whenever one can describe, between a number of statements, such a system of dispersion, whenever, between objects, types of statement, concepts, or thematic choices, one can define a regularity (...), we will say, for the sake of convenience, that we are dealing with a *discursive formation* (...). The conditions to which the elements of this division (objects, modes of statement, concepts, thematic choices) are subjected we shall call the *rules of formation*. The rules of formation are conditions of existence (...) in a given discursive division.' (Foucault 2010 [1969]: 38)

Foucault's interest in such rule-systems is not related to linguistic-grammatical patterns of language use but on the one hand to the semantic level of meanings or the rules of meaning creation, and on the other hand to institutionally embedded stabilized practices of discourse production. Discourse Analysis aims at the reconstruction of the institutionally-practical and symbolically-semantic scarcity mechanisms which lead to the occurrence of specific statements in particular places. Not everything which might be said is actually; and not everything can be said everywhere. The fact is that it is always only one specific type of statement (*énoncés*) that can appear and no other. This may be explained by the rules we have mentioned, which Foucault calls 'rules of formation'. They structure what statements may appear at a particular moment in history at a particular place. These kinds of discursive formations in the sense of his sociology of knowledge perspective, do not refer to the object-related description of extra-discursive objects. The fact is, rather, that they produce them. Archaeology is:

> 'a task that consists of not – no longer – treating discourses as groups of signs (signifying elements referring to contents or representations) but as practices that systematically form the objects of which they speak.' (Foucault 2010 [1969]: 49)

In archaeology the main interest is in the

> 'project of a *pure description of discursive events* as the horizon for the search for the unities that form within it. This description is easily distinguishable from an analysis of the language. Of course, a linguistic

system can be established (...) only by using a corpus of statements, or a collection of discursive facts; but we must then define, on the basis of this grouping, which has value as a sample, rules that may make it possible to construct other statements than these (...). The field of discursive events, on the other hand, is a grouping that is always finite and limited at any moment to the linguistic sequences that have been formulated; they may be innumerable, they may, in sheer size, exceed the capacities of recording, memory, or reading: nevertheless they form a finite grouping. The question posed by language analysis of some discursive fact or other is always: according to what rules has a particular statement been made, and consequently according to what rules could other similar statements be made? The description of the events of discourse poses a quite different question: how is it that one particular statement appeared rather than another? (...) we must grasp the statement in the exact specificity of its occurrence; determine its conditions of existence, fix at least its limits, establish its correlations with other statements that may be connected with it, and show what other forms of statement it excludes.' (Foucault 2010 [1969]: 27–28)

Foucault distinguishes four basic dimensions in discourses which may be analyzed with regard to their formation rules (Foucault 2010: 40ff):

– The *formation of the objects* of a discourse can be discovered through the following (and similar) questions: according to what rules are the objects formed which the discourses are talking about? What scientific disciplines played a role in this? What patterns of classifications are involved?
– The *formation of enunciative modalities* points to questions such as: who is the legitimate speaker, or from what institutional location and subject-position is the discourse object being spoken about? How do the various forms of statement – such as statistics, narrative, experiment and so on – relate to each other?
– The *formation of concepts* refers to questions about the rules that underlie the particular statements: for example, how are the textual elements bound together? What rhetorical schemata are being employed? How are arguments constructed? How is the statement located in the framework of other texts – for example, through the mode of citation? How are quantitative statements translated into qualitative statements?
– The *formation of strategies* aims at the external references of a discourse: what are the themes and theories of the discourse? How do they relate to other discourses? To what extent do they claim to provide better solutions to problems than others? What is the function of a discourse in non-discursive practices?'

From the example of the formation rules it becomes clear how Foucault imagines the operation of archaeological Discourse Analysis: as the fundamental analysis and reconstruction of different levels of production that can be attributed to a statement. It is also clear – for example in the references to the institutional locations that are spoken about, or to professions such as that of a doctor who is authorized to make particular statements, and so on – that Foucault is in no sense looking only at an abstract and somehow 'free floating level' of a text. It is rather the case that with the 'archaeology' he is outlining a comprehensive social science research programme that aims not only at the analysis of statement-contexts but precisely at the social production and order of practices, objects, people, ideas: in brief, the overall contexts of reality:

'If, in clinical discourse, the doctor is in turn the sovereign, direct questioner, the observing eye, the touching finger, the organ that deciphers signs, the point at which previously formulated descriptions are integrated, the laboratory technician, it is because a whole group of relations is involved. Relations between the hospital space as a place of assistance, of purified, systematic observation, and of partially proved, partially experimental therapeutics, and a whole group of perceptual codes of the human body (...) Understood as a renewal of points of view, contents, the forms and even the style of description, the use of inductive or probabilistic reasoning, types of attribution of causality, in short, as a renewal of the modalities of enunciation, clinical medicine must not be regarded as the result of a new technique of observation. (...) but as the establishment of a relation, in medical discourse, between a number of distinct elements, some of which concerned the status of doctors, others the institutional and technical site from which they spoke, others their position as subjects perceiving, observing, describing, teaching, etc.' (Foucault 2010 [1969]: 53)

Advice for Sociological Procedure following Foucault

According to Kendall and Wickham (1999), a Foucauldian perspective implicates:

1 An orientation of search to contingencies instead of cause–effect chains (an historical event is not necessary, but rather a possible result of a series of complex relationships between other events)
2 Not to make use of political arguments or 'second order judgments'. Meaning, introduced reasons that are adopted too easily and unquestioningly (e.g. the effect of class interests or general social structures that lie behind phenomena and determine them)

3 A problem and topic-oriented procedure in the framework of archaeology and genealogy. This procedure should be conducted in a *non-interpretative* way; it is a question of the description of observable regularities, not of the search for deep structures of significance. The concentration on statements replaces a concentration on authors. (Kendall and Wickham 1999: 5ff)

Procedures in Archaeology

There are various proposals for conducting Foucauldian archaeological research. According to Foucault archaeology describes discourses 'as practices specified in the element of the archive' (Foucault 2010: 131). The archive is 'the general system of the formation and transformation of statements' (ibid.: 130) or 'the law of what can be said, the system that governs the appearance of statements as unique events' (ibid: 129). Kendall and Wickham (1999: 26ff) mention seven goals of archaeology:

1 a cartographic description of the relations between what can be said and what can be seen
2 the analysis of relations between statements
3 the formulation of rules for the use of statements
4 the analysis of the positions between speakers with reference to the statements
5 the description of the 'surfaces of emergence' as the places in which objects are referred to and dealt with
6 the description of institutions with authority which define borders for discursive objects
7 the descriptions of 'forms of specification', i.e. the manner in which phenomena are understood and placed in relation to other phenomena.

Maingueneau (1991) names four features of archaeological Discourse Analysis:

1 Archaeological Discourse Analysis 'investigates firstly the *place* of the statement, which means the historically, socially and culturally determined starting point (not: origin) of a series of similar statements. This is the place of legitimized speaking, the place of at least some kind of institutionalization and thus the place of power. This is also a place that the subject must adopt if, within the framework of a discourse, it wishes to say something that will count as true (…)
2 Secondly, Discourse Analysis documents the *registration*, i.e. the statement as a repetition of similar statements. By virtue of this uniformity interrelated statements generate a classification scheme or discursive regularities, and according to this pattern statements are generated within the field of this discourse. (…)

(Continued)

(Continued)

3 Thirdly, Discourse Analysis enquires (...) about the *boundaries* and the *interdiscourse*, i.e. the defining of boundaries, the prohibitions of what may be said, and the connections and mediation elements to other discourses. (...)
4 Fourthly, these three elements constitute, finally, the *archive*, i.e. the possible and in fact, compared to all possible sentences about an object, always 'rare' statements which are stored in the texts of a discursive tradition, and which legitimize a particular present (repeated) type of statement. To investigate a discursive archive – which is, of course, a construction of the analysis – implies examining and ordering the actual statements, using a series of texts; on the basis of this archive one can then make substantial statements about how discourses produce, in all their historical specificity, the social world of what is being designated.' (after Sarasin 2011: 61f).

In the new phase of the development of his work, beginning at the end of the 1960s, Foucault altered the balance of his 'archaeology' programme in favour of the development of a 'genealogy' (Foucault 1977b). This was a further reaction to the criticisms mentioned above of the ahistoricity of structuralist thinking and of its quasi-metaphysical objectivism of structures. While 'archaeology' develops a Discourse Analysis as a photographic snapshot at a particular historical point in time, the genealogical perspective emphasizes the 'process' and action or practice aspects of discourse arrangements and the meaning of power–knowledge complexes.[37] Here we are more concerned with a different accentuation than with a completely new programme: instead of the concentration on systems of statements we find the investigation of practices, by means of which discourses form subjects, but we also find the observation of practices as a relatively autonomous level of reality with its own dynamics or an interplay of the visible (i.e. materializations) and discourses. In this connection we find, for example, the investigations of surveillance and punitive practices (Foucault 1977a), confessional practices, such as confession in church, (Foucault 1988–1990, Vol. 1) or self-disciplinary practices as reported by advisory

---

[37]Admittedly Foucault does not develop any other attempt at a systematic methodological basis for his mode of procedure that might be compared to his 'archaeology'.

books (Foucault 1988–1990, Vol. 2 and 3). What is of central importance here is a specific understanding of power and the relationship between power and knowledge:

'It seems to me that power must be understood in the first instance as the multiplicity of force relations immanent in the sphere in which they operate and which constitute their own organization; as the process which, through ceaseless struggles and confrontations, transforms and strengthens, or reverses them (...); and lastly, as the strategies in which they take effect, whose general design or institutional crystallization is embodied in the state apparatus, in the formulation of the law, in the various social hegemonies. (...) Power (...) is the name that one attributes to a complex strategical situation in a particular society. (...) Relations of power are not in a position of exteriority with respect to other types of relationships (economic processes, knowledge relationships, sexual relations), but are immanent in the latter.' (Foucault 1998 [1976]: 92–94)

Example of an historical Discourse Analysis using Michel Foucault's approach

Philipp Sarasin: Short-tempered Machines

'I would rather show precisely what happens when an influential discourse begins to say: "this is a body which operates in such a way, which you can regulate in this way, which is exposed to these kinds of dangers and which offers you these kinds of pleasures." In other words: this book attempts to provide a historical context for the obvious sentence, "I have a body", and I will argue that the modern way of speaking about one's own body – the body of the subject – was first developed in the context of the discourse on hygiene in the 19th century (...). How, when and where did it originate, this modern way in which individuals, as speaking and acting subjects, relate to their own body? (...) What objects appear in it? What categories does it make available, with which the citizens whom it addresses as subjects could perceive themselves as corporeal beings? (...) At the centre of the hygiene discourse there is the belief that individuals largely have it in their hands to determine their health, sickness or even the time of their death (...).' (Sarasin 2001: 18f.)

In his inaugural speech to the Parisian *Collège de France* in December 1970, Foucault expands on the idea already introduced in the 'archaeology' concerning the explanation of the formation rules of discourse, that discourses are directly connected to enabling and exclusion criteria. Included in this are, for example, academic grades or the textual genres of (critical) reviewing. These criteria distinguish possible legitimate speakers from non-legitimate speakers; thus, they constitute subject-positions. As with statements, the amount of possible speakers is subject to a range of processes of rarefaction, for instance by means of qualification rituals, comment-procedures that assess the value of statements in discourses, true–false judgments that select 'results' that are worth preserving, and so on. Following Nietzsche, for Foucault too human history appears to be a sequence of contingent constellations and interpretations, whose temporary stabilization is the result of power struggles. What in specific historical contexts counts as truth is only an assertion within a particular language or 'truth' game:

> 'Truth is a thing of this world: it is produced only by virtue of multiple forms of constraint. And it induces regular effects of power. Each society has its regime of truth, its "general politics" of truth: that is, the types of discourse which it accepts and makes function as true; the mechanisms and instances which enable one to distinguish true and false statements, the means by which each is sanctioned; the techniques and procedures accorded value in the acquisition of truth; the status of those who are charged with saying what counts as true. (Foucault 1984: 72–73) '"Genealogy" thus results in a "history of truth": Not a history that would be concerned with what might be true in the fields of learning, but an analysis of the "games of truth", the games of truth and error through which being is historically constituted as experience; that is, as something that can and must be thought. What are the games of truth by which man proposes to think its own nature when he perceives himself to be mad; when he considers himself to be ill; when he conceives of himself as a living, speaking, laboring being; when he judges and punishes himself as a criminal?' (Foucault 1992 [1984]: 6–7)

With the French term *dispositif* (often translated as 'apparatus') Foucault now characterizes the interwoven bundle of 'means and measures' – including persons, objects, organisations, rules, proceedings and the like – that are the basics for the production of a specific discourse and/or for the production of a discourse's power effects, its interventions into the world.[38] These include laws, architectural manifestations, such as the construction of prisons (Bentham's 'Panopticon'), speech practices such as confession and so on. *Practices*, i.e. routinized or institutionalized patterns of behaviour and action, are generally given a new value. This is valid not only for discursive (i.e. linguistic) and non-discursive practices (such as symbolically loaded gestures) within a dispositif, but also for the practices of addressees (frequently stubborn and self-perpetuating) which possess a specific routinized meaning for those social actors that frequently does not correspond with the expectations of the discourses. In *Discipline and Punish* (Foucault 1977) and then above all in his investigations into the relationship between sexuality and truth in *The History of Sexuality* (Foucault 1988–1990), Foucault was concerned with the effects of power–knowledge complexes, that is to say, supra-subjective orders of knowledge on meaning attributions, the bodies and the practices of human subjects (Foucault 1988b).[39]

'One example of this link between modes of behaviour, interpretations of actors and collective orders of knowledge is provided by the bodily healthcare practices of the late classical society that are extensively analysed by Foucault in *Le Souci de Soi* (vol. 3 of *L'Histoire de la sexualité*). These – non-discursive – practices, at a preliminary level, consist of observable physical modes of behaviour that are to do with a "careful" and health-conscious way of dealing with one's own body. These modes of behavior can in no sense be taken for granted; their production assumes, rather, a particular piece of supra-subjective knowledge formation that in a general sense determines that the body is an object

---

[38]The term *dispositif* is common in French. It refers to a collection of measures (such as laws, ordinances, official responsibilities, material objects) that are prepared, for example, for a political, economic or technical purpose. Several authors are working on how one might further shape *dispositif* analysis in other senses (see Bührmann and Schneider 2008).

[39]Foucault is reproached for having neglected, in his idea of disciplinary power, the arbitrariness, power of resistance and cunning of individuals/subjects in the face of such demands. For that reason Giddens, for example, contrasts Goffman's analyses of this kind of potential as a corrective in the investigation of whole institutions (Giddens 1986). Even though Foucault was primarily interested in disciplinary processes, he still sees very clearly the 'other side', as is made clear by his statements in this connection, and by his political commitment (Eribon 1992; Foucault 1988b, 2002; Dreyfus and Rabinow 1982).

of individual "care", a precarious phenomenon that needs to be constantly protected. This general body-code provides the background for quite different modes of behaviour, which would not be intelligible or explicable, if they were not the result of a generally shared meaning-pattern. (...) What is decisive to understand "practices" in Foucault's later action-theory knowledge analysis is the fact that the questionable knowledge code cannot be located at the level of self-reproducing discourses but rather appears as incorporated in the actors who produce the practices and constantly interpret their own action-environment, which of course includes themselves.' (Reckwitz 2000: 298f)

Guidelines for a Genealogical
Discourse Analysis, following Foucault

Carabine (2001) proposes eleven steps of a genealogical approach to discourse:

1 Selection of the research object and investigation of relevant data sources
2 Making acquaintance with the data (through repeated reading)
3 Identification of themes, categories and objects of the discourse
4 Search for evidence of inter-discursive relationships
5 Identify the discursive strategies and techniques that are employed
6 Search for what is not being said and for gaps
7 Search for resistances and counter-discourses
8 Identify the effects of the discourse
9 Context 1: Sketch the background to the object
10 Context 2: Contextualize the material in the power/knowledge networks of the particular history period
11 Pay attention to the limitations of the research, the data and the sources

(following Carabine 2001: 281ff)

Foucault was influential both through his material investigations and also his analytic concepts. Admittedly this did not lead to any theoretically or methodologically consistently developed proposal for the conduct of analyses of discourse, either for Foucault himself or for the many studies that relied on 'his methodology'. The few analytical threads that have been introduced here make clear the heterogeneity but also the relative generality of the proposals in question; this is particularly true of his dealing with empirical material. In the secondary and research literature that relates to Foucault we may find, with regard to methodological implementations, predominantly terminological and theoretical explanations for conceptualization, but almost no hints – at least from the perspective of qualitative social research, nothing satisfactory – about concrete strategies for the processing of material. Reference to Foucault, therefore, has little to say about actual methodological procedures.

Post-Marxist Discourse Theory: Ernesto Laclau and Chantal Mouffe

Since the mid-1980s the political scientists Chantal Mouffe and Ernesto Laclau have published a range of contributions to a post-Marxist and post-structuralist theory of discourse. They relate to ideas of Foucault's, and even more strongly to Althusser's ideology theory (see above), Gramsci's notion of hegemony (see above) and Lacan's theory of the subject (Lacan 2007). In the process they develop discourse theory into a general social theory of the construction of individual and collective identities. In the end they identify discourses with the 'social' *per se*: according to Laclau and Mouffe the 'social', or society, exists always and essentially as something symbolic, that is, as an order of meaning.

The Discourse Theory of Ernesto Laclau and Chantal Mouffe

Brief surveys and introductions into the discourse theory of Mouffe and Laclau are to be found in Howarth (2000: 101ff; Howarth 2009), Jørgensen and Philipps (2002: 24ff), Andersen (2003), Nonhoff (2006, 2007). Torfing (1999) provides a comprehensive survey of the development and the discourse-theory conception of the approach. Applications are predominantly to be found in the political science context. He discusses analyses of the link between nationalism and racism, and mass media and the welfare state. Further applications to environmental policy, apartheid discourses in South Africa or racist and homophobic discourses in England are to be found in Howarth, Norval and Stavrakakis (2000); the papers in Howarth and Torfing

(Continued)

(2005) relate to questions of the formation of political identity in Europe. Nonhoff (2006) analyses the German discourse on the social market economy. David Howarth, Jakob Torfing, Louise Phillips, Marianne Jørgensen and others are currently concerned with developing a stronger methodological foundation for the approach. In German-speaking countries relevant papers are to be found in the journal *kulturRevolution*.

These symbolic orders include both concrete material objects and also modes of action, or practices and subject-positions for human actors. The links between the elements in this order are produced and stabilized by meaning attributions; every social practice is always a practice of meaning-creation, irrespective of whether it is to do with the production of an object, with a bodily movement, or speaking – everything becomes a signifier, even where there is no explicit intention to transmit a sign or to communicate. The orders of meaning we have mentioned are constituted by means of discourses. Discourses are systems of forming differences, that is, of internal and outward-looking delimitations that are temporarily stabilized at the social and institutional levels. They aim to reduce, fix and stabilize the meaning-excess, the infinite multiplicity of possible modes of interpretation that is inherent in any use of signs and thus to invoke current, accepted and shared modes of interpretation. Such processes for the fixing of meaning take place in the practices of 'articulation' by social actors; the latter can thereby stabilize, challenge and change discourses (Laclau and Mouffe 1985; Laclau 1977, 1990, 1993, 1994, 1996).

The discourse-immanent formations of differences that we have mentioned are not determined by an objective meaning structure but are the (contested) result of the articulation practices of social actors and subjects. Within a discourse, delimitations take place according to a *logic of difference*: individual components take their significance and their meaning in relation to the structure of discourse-internal differentiations. For instance, if a discourse applies to the 'Unity of the Nation', then it can be internally structured by differentiations which separate the 'leaders' (the head) from the supporting other 'organs', which allocate specific roles to men and women, and so on. Through the *logic of equivalence* these kinds of discourse-internal differentiations are again unified; this happens while a discourse tries to build up its frontier with 'the external other(s)': in a situation of war, for example, there are no longer any dominators or dominated, no workers and rulers, but only a people, a fatherland and 'the enemies'. Laclau (1996: 36ff) suggests the term 'empty signifier' for this kind of unifying sign, which ultimately seeks to characterize the overall identity of the discourse. As an example of this he considers the value of the word 'freedom', which is used as an abstract cipher that can be charged with different meanings, when it is a matter of acting in the name of freedom or the free world against an external other (such as: the communist block; the 'Axis of Evil'; 'rogue states').

What are described as *hegemonial* are discourses that tend to develop a comprehensive picture of the world and within it to classify all social relations in an overall structure. However, this is rather a matter of a tendency to 'hegemoniality'; the texture of orders of meanings is always characterized by antagonisms and surpluses of meaning, by breaches, conflicts and so on. Therefore, they are always 'in motion'. Of course discourses offer more or less fixed subject positions, but subjects are always at the intersection of a number of varied discourses, and thus also varied subject positions (e.g. man, white-man, Western European, Frenchman, Parisian, minister).[40] Subjects relate to such a range of possible positions in various processes of identification: subjectivity manifests itself, according to Laclau, following Lacan and his concept of 'desire', in the process of deciding in situations where – in terms of the available criteria – no guidelines or orientation markers for decisions exist (Stäheli 1999: 155).

> 'The inconclusiveness of discourses, i.e. the impossibility of ever achieving a complete identity, repeatedly leads to situations in which the deficiency in the discourse comes to light in the form of things that cannot be decided. Whereas a traditional conception of subject in such cases would use a more or less rationally deciding subject that is confronted to problems of decision-making, Laclau's option is quite different: no subject exists that is independent of the impossibility of deciding, which has to be resolved through his/her decision. The subject comes into being, rather, in the course of *identification* with a particular content that is supposed to solve the "undecidable" situation (...) If a new imaginary is offered in England through *New Labour* or in Germany through the *Neue Mitte*, and this is supposed to "sew" a critical situation (...), then the contingency of this political opportunity depends on the suppression of alternative areas of identification (such as "Old

[40]The relationship of the idea of subject-positions, also found in Althusser and Foucault, to the sociological concept of roles receives little attention (Stäheli 2000: 48f).

Labour" or neoliberalism). The moment of the subject does not consist in complete identification with "New Labour" but in that moment of undecidability in which identification has not yet taken place. This "not yet" should not be understood simply in a temporal sense, but as an indication that every identification fails, since the subject is never completely taken up by his identification (...) The successful realization of an identification leads to the consolidation of subject positions and *thereby* to the obliteration of the moment of the subject (...). For subject positions are produced by means of the successful temporary resolution of situations of undecidability.' (Stäheli 1999: 155f)

The discourse theory of Laclau and Mouffe, which has been briefly discussed here, led to a *Theory of the Political as the Social Arrangement of Articulation Practices*. More recently it has also become the basis of a number of discourse research projects which, as yet, contain very little guidance on methodology.

Cultural Studies, Feminist Theory, Post-colonialism

Finally we must mention here the three different but partly overlapping lines of discussion found in Cultural Studies, Feminist Theory and Post-colonial Studies. They have not developed any independent discourse theories, but because of the questions they ask and the early intensive reception of French Post-structuralism and, above all, Foucault's works, they inspired and marked the present-day boom in discourse research in essential ways. As a rapidly expanding discipline in the present day, Cultural Studies (e.g. in the different approaches of Stuart Hall and John Fiske), and the closely related theories of Post-colonialism, have become associated with semiotics, Structuralism and Post-structuralism in fundamental ways.[41]

Studies in Post-colonialism investigate the link between material and symbolic-cultural consequences of the power structures of Colonialism, for example in relation to the western European conception of 'others', the ideas of definable

---

[41]On this see Barker (2000), During (2005), the contributions in Hepp and Winter (1999), Hörning and Winter (1999) and Hall (1980, 1991, 1997); for a comparison of the approaches of Hall and Fiske, and the influences of Laclau and Mouffe and Foucault, see Winter (1999; 2000), and more specifically on John Fiske, Winter and Mikos (2001); Keller (2005a).

cultural identities and the development of transnational and hybrid ways of living. In his classic study of the western European construction of hegemonial ideas of 'the Orient', Edward W. Said makes use of Foucault's theoretical conceptions of discourse to reconstruct the genesis and implementation of corresponding stereotypes of 'western' and 'eastern' in research into the Orient and western literature.[42]

Within Cultural Studies the coming together of 'Culturalism' – i.e. the theory and investigation especially of British working-class culture as a practice – and Semiotics or Structuralism led to the development of a variety of comprehensive theories of the social process as a permanent production and transformation of symbolic and material orders (Hall 1980), but this has not so far resulted in greater systematic developments in discourse-analytical perspectives. In this work there are frequent references to semiotic and (post)structuralist discourse models or to the discourse theory of Laclau and Mouffe.[43] Cultural Studies sees the circulation of meanings (especially in the mass media) as powerful struggles for symbolic orders; in this they emphasize the actual processes, that is to say, the articulation practice of sign-production and the wide variety of different types of meaning adaptation by recipients. In more recent proposals for Discourse Analysis coming out of Cultural Studies, referring specifically to concrete work on text, there has been a preference for the procedures of semiotics or those of Critical Discourse Analysis, which was mentioned above (Barker and Galasinski 2001; Hepp 1999: 262ff).

Finally, discourse theory ideas emanating from French Post-structuralism had already enjoyed a broad reception in Feminist Theory at a very early stage and exerted an influence on the development of research in Women's and Gender Studies (Hekman 1996). Following Foucault, the discursive processes involved in the creation of sex/gender, its relation to the material aspect of bodies and its social situation became a major topic in the works of authors such as Judith Butler (1990, 1993), Gayatri C. Spivak (1990), and others. In Germany, Bublitz (1998) and Bührmann (1995), for example, interpreted the social and biological orders of the sexes as a difference-structure that is

---

[42]Apart from Edward Said (1979), Homi Bhabba and Gayatri C. Spivak are important authors in the Post-colonialism debate. On this see Mills (1997: 105ff), Howarth (2000: 68ff) and Gandhi (1998).

[43]It remains controversial to what extent Cultural Studies or Post-colonialist Approaches 'fulfil' Foucault's concept of discourse; see Kendall and Wickham (1999).

produced and hierarchized by discourse practice. They also investigated its genesis, reproduction mechanisms and transformation potential: [44]

'While semiotic approaches concentrate in a narrower sense on the investigation of processes of meaning and interpretation, discourse-oriented modes of access within feminist theory place in the foreground the production of knowledge, for instance of sexual differences, and the question of how this knowledge is rooted in social practices and institutions that determine the relationship between the genders, as well as in experienced subjectivities' (Hark 2011: 362).

Discourse, Gender and Bodies

Feminist social scientists have reconstructed, for example, what implicit gender models underlie the 'relevant' scientific discourses of the eighteenth and nineteenth centuries, what ideas of gender and gender relations are embedded in the scientific and medical writings of early modern times and the present day, and how they have caused changes in the public perceptions of the female body (Maihofer 1995). In her essay on the 'female body as a public place', Barbara Duden (1991) formulates the following research interest in the reception of specific discourses:

'I want to investigate the conditions under which, in the course of one generation, new techniques and modes of speaking have turned our understanding and experience of pregnancy upside down. For in the course of a few years the **child** became a **foetus**, a pregnant woman became a **uterine supply system**, the unborn child became a **life**, and the "life" became a **secular-catholic** (i.e. all-embracing) **value**. (...) I am pursuing the question of the extent to which since the eighteenth century the scientific fact of "woman" has been so produced and popularized that I experience it in myself. (...) What I seek to understand is the corporeal self-production of the woman in two processes that condition each other: on the one hand in the internalization of scientific concepts, and on the other in the self-attribution of technogenic images' (Duden 1991: 10ff)

---

[44]Important stages and references in the formation of feminist theory are documented in McNay (1992), Mills (1997), Naples (2003), Hark (2011, 2005), Becker-Schmidt and Knapp (2000), Raab (1998), Knapp and Wetterer (1992), Maihofer (1995) and Wobbe and Lindeman (1994). Studies are abounding (e.g. Schiebinger 2004, the works of Evelyn Fox Keller and many others).

2.7 Sociology of Knowledge Approach to Discourse

In the Sociology of Knowledge Approach to Discourse (SKAD) we are concerned with a discourse research perspective that finds its origin in the sociology of knowledge theory of Peter Berger and Thomas Luckmann, and builds a bridge between the Culturalist Approaches to discourse research mentioned above and the Discourse Theories that have been presented, in particular those of Foucault (Keller 1998, 2005a, b, 2010, 2011a,b, 2012, forthcoming).[45] Both traditions are based on the assumption that everything we perceive, experience, sense is mediated through socially constructed and typified knowledge (e.g. schemata of meanings, interpretations and actions) – a knowledge, that is, to varying degrees, recognized as legitimate and 'objective'. We have no direct access to the world *per se*, even when its material quality sets up obstacles before us and confronts us with problems of interpretation, in other words, allows the 'robustness of knowledge' room for manoeuvre (Pickering 1995; Hacking 2000). Our knowledge of the world cannot be traced back to an innate cognitive system of categories but to socially created symbolic systems that are produced in and through discourses. The Sociology of Knowledge Approach to Discourse investigates these social practices and processes of communicative construction, stabilization and transformation of symbolic orders and their consequences: for example, laws, statistics, classifications, techniques, objects and practices are, in this sense, effects of discourses and the 'pre'-conditions for new discourses. SKAD is then concerned with reconstructing processes of social construction, objectivization, communication and legitimization of meaning structures (i.e. structures of interpretation

---

[45]The basic idea of the Sociology of Knowledge Approach to Discourse is explained more fully in my works listed above and in the methodological chapters below. Certain more recent sociological discourse analyses also formulate ideas on a mediation between sociology of knowledge and Foucault, even if they do not use the label I have suggested and do not develop this perspective systematically. Elements of the Sociology of Knowledge Approach to Discourse are to be found in investigations such as those of Hajer (1995), Waldschmidt (1996), Schneider (1999), Schwab-Trapp (2010, 2011), Viehöver (2005), Knoblauch (1995, 2006), Christmann (2004), van Dyk (2006) and papers in Keller, Hirseland, Schneider and Viehöver (2010). Keller and Truschkat (2012) present several studies drawing on SKAD. Gusfield's study on 'Drunken Driving' may be read as a classical example of this kind of perspective. In a different (that is: linguistic) disciplinary context Dietrich Busse (1987), in his 'Historical Semantics', was aiming at an inter-connection between different traditions in the Sociology of Knowledge.

and action) at the level of institutions and organizations or social (collective) actors, and with analysing the social effects of such processes. This includes a variety of dimensions of reconstruction: those of meaning production and those of action/practices, institutional, structural and material contexts as well as social consequences. Actors formulate the communicated components out of which discourses unfold; in this they orientate themselves in their (discursive) practices according to the available resources and the rules of the particular fields of discourse.

The conception and name of the Sociology of Knowledge Approach to Discourse are bound up with two intentions: in the first place this expresses the fact that sociological discourse research is concerned with questions and phenomena that belong with the area of the sociology of knowledge. This is to do with expanding the theoretical bases and research perspectives of sociological or sociology-of-knowledge hermeneutics. In the second place this makes it possible to link discourse research to the established discussion and to develop qualitative methods of social research within this paradigm. This kind of undertaking seems both useful and essential in a number of respects: for example, 'Hermeneutic Sociology of Knowledge' (Hitzler, Reichertz and Schröer 1999b; Schröer 1994, 1997; Hitzler and Honer 1997) provides a theory of social knowledge-production, institutional stabilization of supplies of knowledge and knowledge acquisition. The interpretative paradigm has also served to bring the categories of actors and their actions back into Discourse Analysis. To this must be added a progressive reflection on processes of understanding and opening up qualitative data from an interpretative and hermeneutic point of view.

German Sociology of Knowledge of recent decades has been primarily oriented to microanalyses of knowledge and has focused neither on the social knowledge-production in scientific fields nor on the careers of public discourses as processes in the constitution and circulation of knowledge.[46] The investigation of such phenomena, however, undoubtedly is one of the objects of a comprehensive sociology-of-knowledge perspective. Here the works of Foucault in particular have provided important suggestions concerning the powerful institutional mechanisms of the circulation of knowledge and in addition – from the viewpoint of their later questions – concerning the

---

[46] The first of these has been primarily the concern of laboratory studies in the context of research in science and technology; the latter was the subject of a number of culturalist analyses and a range of investigations of the career of public problems.

meaning of practices in this process. The orientation on Foucault, Bourdieu and others can therefore assist in the correction of the micro-sociological and situative bias of the interpretative paradigm and the adoption of a broader analytical perspective that takes account of social and historical contexts.[47]

Berger and Luckmann (1975 [1966]), in their work on the 'Social Construction of Reality', formulated a basic theory of the social production, objectivization, circulation and adaptation of knowledge, bringing together a variety of social science traditions – American Pragmatism and Symbolic Interactionism, Alfred Schütz's Social Phenomenology (1967) – and traditions of 'objectivist' knowledge analysis (Emile Durkheim, Karl Marx).[48] In this a co-constitutionalist conception of the interactive creation of knowledge (e.g. via typification), of its social objectification and the subjective-socializing adaptation of knowledge is developed. Berger and Luckmann concentrate on the everyday, basic stocks of knowledge of members of society. They state quite explicitly that they are not interested in particular or specialized social knowledge.[49] This bias, which is not necessarily connected to their conception, may be corrected through the use of a Sociology of Knowledge Approach to Discourse.

SKAD is concerned with processes and practices of the production and circulation of knowledge at the level of the institutional fields (such as sciences or the public domain) in modern societies. In this, discourses are seen as analytically definable ensembles of practices and meaning attributions. The relation between the individual discourse event and the whole discourse may therefore be formulated, using Anthony Giddens' concept of 'duality of

---

[47]I cannot discuss here the parallels with the discourse ideas of Fairclough, and Laclau and Mouffe. But in general terms, in the current debate, the perspectives of the phenomenologically based sociology of knowledge of Berger and Luckmann – in the tradition of pragmatic semiotics – seem to converge with those of post-structuralist semiotics. See Keller (2005a).

[48]For an overview and the full context see Keller (2009).

[49]In this respect their approach later on also underlies developments in Sociology-of-Knowledge Hermeneutics: 'The goal is to (re-)construct on the basis of what meaning relations human beings act, how they act. They ask how subjects, born into a world historically and socially filled with meanings, permanently interpret and thus also change this world. To be precise: it is a matter of the (re)construction of the processes with which acting subjects can repeatedly "find themselves anew" in an historically established and given social world. This also means: how they find their way and how, in the process, they simultaneously create this world "anew" and change it.' (Reichertz and Schröer 1994: 59)

structure' (Giddens 1986) as actualization, reproduction or transformation of a discourse structure that only exists in this performing actualization. In the words of Pierre Bourdieu this sort of structure is simultaneously both structured – that is, the result of past processes of 'structure-formation' – and structuring, with regard to the scope of future discursive events. The methodological richness of sociology permits a broader empirical underpinning of discourse research than is possible in approaches rooted in linguistics or discourse theory. This expansion consists primarily of the possibility of disengagement from the 'text', but also of the use of additional meaning-oriented methods of reconstruction. Thus, the investigation of the semantic and symbolic content of discursively processed knowledge and interpretation inventories, in more or less far-reaching analyses from the synchronic or diachronic viewpoint, also constitutes the core of SKAD. As an empirical social science, however, it can make accessible the practices of discourse production not only through texts, but can observe them more or less *in actu*, including their rules and (unequally divided) resources, the role of collective actors, the concrete-situative conditions, and the social contexts that go beyond these.

Meanwhile in the German-speaking world (and beyond) many studies use the Sociology of Knowledge Approach to Discourse as their starting point (Keller and Truschkat 2012). These include investigations of environmental discourses (Keller 1998), analyses of spatial construction (Christmann 2004), of health discourses (Bechmann 2007), competence discourses and practice (Truschkat 2008), identity construction in leftist social movements during the Israel-Palestine conflict (Ullrich 2008), the media construction of Satanism (Schmied-Knittel 2008), American self-reassurance on family models in discourses on same-sex partnerships (Zimmermann 2009), education policy discourses on innovation (Bormann 2009), criminological questions (Singelnstein 2009), identity formation of families of Chinese migrant communities in Romania (Wundrak 2010), or the political-science construction of the 'knowledge object of suicide bombing' (Brunner 2010). Starting from SKAD, the studies each take up particular questions and associated concrete conceptualizations or links to other perspectives.[50]

---

[50]The 'Situational Analysis' of Adele Clarke (2005) shares with SKAD a number of assumptions, in particular the link between the Interpretative Paradigm and Foucault's Discourse Theory; in its analytical interests it focuses on the grounded theory paradigm, which is elaborated far beyond its classical versions, towards the analysis of situations. There are many convergences between Situational Analysis and SKAD.

The procedures of empirical discourse research in the social sciences explained below in Chapters 3–6 were elaborated in the late 1990s; they are oriented to the programme of a comprehensive analysis of social knowledge relations and knowledge policy, as it has been formulated through the Sociology of Knowledge Approach to Discourse since then.

2.8 Further Disciplinary Developments

Apart from the sociological, historical and discourse-linguistic approaches and the different discourse-theory perspectives so far mentioned, in recent years empirical discourse research has also undergone a rapid development. In addition, we may give here a number of further indications of corresponding uses of the discourse perspective.

In the political sciences there is tension between discourse perspectives that tend to favour the Habermas tradition and view discourses as argumentation processes that may play a role in 'negotiations' – or may not (if non-argumentative power resources are applied in decision-making). Against this long-standing opposition between 'arguing' and 'bargaining' (Prittwitz 1996), which extends into the more recent Discursive Institutionalism of Vivian Schmidt (2009), there are positions that start much more fundamentally with the discursive constitution of the particular fields of decision. Relevant political science approaches with a more or less strong linguistic and sociological base are explained in Maas (1988, 1989), Januschek (1985), Fischer and Forester (1993), Fischer and Gottweis (2012), Hajer (1995, 2002, 2010), Donati (2011), Chilton and Schaffner (2002), Mottier (2002), Howarth and Torfing (2005), Kerchner and Schneider (2006), with reference to Critical Discourse Analysis in Fairclough and Fairclough (2012). The international network on Interpretive Policy Analysis with its annual conferences today presents a major arena for discussion of Discourse Analysis in policy studies; the online-journal *Criticial Policy Analysis* is one important arena of discussion.

Meanwhile, discourse perspectives have also found a strong place in Educational Studies, where, in particular, institutional educational discourses and the school as a place of discursive practice have come under scrutiny (e.g. Rogers 2011; Ricken 2006; Wrana 2006; Grochla 2008; Langer 2008; Truschkat 2008; Jäckle 2008). In Human Geography and in sociological Spatial Research there are increasing numbers of discourse studies.

There are repeated contributions in the journal *Urban Studies* and others (see Jacobs 2006) or – admittedly very selectively and not reproducing the broad scope of the discussion – in the handbook by Glasze and Mattissek (2009), as well as the studies by Christmann (e.g. Christmann 2004 on the city image of Dresden). There is also the work of Modan (2007), presenting ethnographic discourse-research in an African-American neighbourhood in an American city, and further ideas about the use of discourse-analytical perspectives in spatial research can be found in Marxhausen (2010), and, in more general terms, in Christmann's (2013) work on broader communication, knowledge and discourse-oriented perspectives. An important focus of contemporary discourse research is also provided by questions that connect the interests of Biographical Research to the analytical resources of the discourse perspective (for example, in the work of Gabriele Rosenthal; see Völter, Dausien, Lutz and Rosenthal 2009). In addition, see also the study by Freitag (2005) on the biographical experience of 'Thalidomide-damage', or the already mentioned study by Wundrak (2010) on processes of identity formation of Chinese migrants in Romania. Similarly, the questions of the relationship between discourse research and ethnography is now being more seriously discussed (Keller, 2003, 2005a; Modan 2007; Langer 2008).

Finally we should mention a number of more recent interdisciplinary collections that look at the Discourse Analysis of the economy (Diaz-Bone and Krell 2010), the relationship between discourse, power and the subject (Keller, Schneider and Viehöver 2012), the relationship between discourse and governmentality (Angermüller and van Dyk 2010), or questions of 'discursive change' (Landwehr 2010). Clarke (2005) extends classical *Grounded Theory* and moves it 'around the postmodern turn' to include concepts from discourse theory and Discourse Analysis.

2.9 Summary

This overview of the various approaches in discourse research has shown that the use of the term 'discourse' includes the microscopic analysis of small conversational and textual extracts in the context of Discourse Analysis and also the diachronic analysis of semantic shifts in linguistic discourse history or the totally non-concrete, abstracting analysis of historical 'orders of discourse' that uses the Discourse Theories of Foucault, or Mouffe and Laclau. In view of this actual and irrevocable heterogeneity in the use of the term, it makes little sense to make an easy distinction here between 'correct' and 'incorrect' discourse perspectives. What is decisive for the usefulness of the term discourse is rather the respective suitability and the justified use that is made of it with regard to specific research interests. Whether the present-day boom in discourse research will lead to the formation of Discourse Studies as an independent interdisciplinary field, as van Dijk (1997c) assumes, or whether instead its base in questions of the particular background disciplines gives it all its vitality and fertility, is not a matter of concern to us in the present context.

To summarize, in linguistic and historical-science contexts comparatively elaborated methodological procedures for qualitative analysis have been developed – for example in Discourse Analysis, CDA, *Kritische Diskursanalyse* – on the one hand, and quantitative analyses of discourse – for example in Corpus Linguistics or Historical Discourse Research – on the other hand, for specific research interests. In contrast to this the *Discourse Theories* of Foucault or Mouffe and Laclau, or their empirical applications, have been very restrained in respect of their methodological implementation. Admittedly, against the background of the sociological approaches of Culturalist Discourse Research, the affinities and convergence of the different approaches to the social production of symbolic orders can be seen. From this, links can then be made, within the framework of the Sociology of Knowledge Approach to Discourse, to qualitative social research and the methodological developments taking place there. In the following chapters, with regard to social sciences research interests, important basic categories and questions of discourse research will be introduced and possible methodological and practical research procedures will then be explained.

THREE

The Research Process

Every discourse research project first needs a clarification of its discourse theory basis. Here the approaches that were introduced in Chapter 2 all have different proposals to make. Having established such a theoretical location, methodological reflections concerning the 'fit' of research questions, data material and methods follow. Only then, or in a discussion of these, do we find the concrete empirical-methodological implementation of a research project. Discourse research is characterized by an essential reflexivity of which it should be aware: it does not produce truth, but 'statement events' which are themselves part of a (social science) discourse. As a scientific discourse about discourses it in turn underlies processes of social structuring, i.e. specifically situated possibilities and constraints on the production of statements – for example in respect of the transparency of methodological steps – and these can then be made the object of further observation. In the preceding explanation of programmes in Discourse Analysis and discourse theory, we gave several indications of the stages and methods involved in empirical implementation. The concrete procedure differs considerably between the various approaches outlined above. The following proposals for the methodological structure and implementation of social science discourse research are based on the framework of the *Sociology of Knowledge Approach to Discourse* (SKAD), that is to say, in the connection between culturalist and discourse theory perspectives that is embedded in the Sociology of Knowledge (Keller 2011b, 2012). This perspective emphasizes the inevitability of a hermeneutic-interpretative stance in the research process, but by virtue of the link to social science hermeneutics (Hitzler and Honer 1997) it aims at a certain degree of transparency and accountability of work on a text. The following proposals are not intended as rigid prescriptions but as guidelines for orientation in the context of a more extensive open project in the discussion of methodologies. They can and indeed must be adapted, further developed and/or supplemented in the research process.[1]

3.1 Concepts

In modern societies social *actors* are bound up in many ways in discursively structured symbolic battles about definitions of reality. This is true not only of processes of public debate but also, for example, as social studies of science have shown (Latour 1987), in the intra-disciplinary production and dissemination of knowledge. Here it is a matter of determining what is actually the case, and of political, moral or aesthetic criteria for the evaluation. The participating actors employ symbolic and cultural devices to create an audience for their narratives: widespread metaphors, well-known narrative patterns, images and so on. SKAD (Keller 2005a; 2011a [2001], 2011b, 2012, forthcoming) investigates processes of the 'social construction of reality' – the 'objectivity of orders and their communicative construction' (Sprondel 1994) – in institutional domains of society. For this it requires basic conceptual distinctions: it is interested in discourses as finite, situated meaning-constituting events, or practices of the use of language and signs by social actors, unfolding around 'thematic or institutional references'. The concept of 'practice' plays a role in discourse research in a number of different respects: a distinction is made between discursive and non-discursive practices of discourse-production, practices as discourse-effects, and practices as a level of reality independent of discourse. The different categories may be illustrated with examples in tabular form:

---

[1]I shall not elaborate separately here on the procedures found in the other approaches mentioned above (see the literature given in the relevant sections). For social science discourse research, detailed linguistic questions and methods are of lesser importance, or are only relevant in the context of interdisciplinary cooperation.

Practices	of Discourse-Production	as Discourse-Effects	as a level of their own, more or less independent of discourse
discursive	e.g. writing, lecturing, preaching, producing analyses	e.g. medical diagnoses, consultation talks	everyday conversations
non-discursive	e.g. symbolic gestures (blessing); wearing specific clothes, demonstrating (walking in the streets)	e.g. sorting domestic, refuse; specific hygiene practices	e.g. punishment routines, traditionally passed on learned routines of everyday action and behaviour

In addition to the form and content-related rules of communicative processes in institutional domains, distributions of resources play an important role in the participation in the communicative exchange and in the content that may be formulated. This may be encapsulated in two sentences:

- *Who* may legitimately speak *where*?
- *What* can/may be said and *how*?

Discourses do not map 'the world' but constitute reality in a specific way. The social actors, who show themselves as speakers in discourses, who occupy the positions of speakers and sometimes form explicit or implicit discourse coalitions, have at their disposal various unequally shared resources for articulation and the production of resonance. In addition to being actualized in the linguistic practices of discourse production, discourses are stabilized by means of *dispositifs* – institutionalized infrastructural elements and assemblages of measures (such as areas of responsibility, formal procedures, objects, technologies, sanctions, educational procedures and so on). On the one hand these may contribute to the (re)production of a discourse, and on the other hand through them a discourse may 'intervene in the world' and therefore realize power-effects.[2] Discourses not only produce

---

[2]A *dispositif* may also include the formal, institutionally legitimized texts that indicate how to proceed in specific cases of application (such as laws, regulations, legal prescriptions and so on). For example, in the discussion of waste disposal, various sub-departments of the federal office for the Environment, including the statistical offices who record the occurrence of waste, belong to the discourse-producing *dispositif*, while waste disposal vehicles, rubbish bins and other phenomena mark the aspect of 'world-intervention'. This is not a matter of a strict separation, but of a different accentuation in respect of discourses.

the *meaning-structures* of our reality, and thus in a certain sense, reality itself, but they have other real effects. The relationship between discourse and the individual discursive event may be understood, as mentioned above, in terms of the concept of 'duality of structure' formulated by Giddens (1986), as a recursive relationship: discourses exist only insofar as they are realized by social actors. Simultaneously they form the precondition for this realization. Following Foucault, I use the term 'utterance' ('énonciation') to refer to the concrete isolated unique statement-event. In contrast 'statement' (énoncé) already means the first level of the typical: the same statement can be found in quite different statement-events or utterances and situative contexts. In the same way, not every speech act or speech event – for instance a greeting – is always a component of a discourse simply because it is ritualized and institutionalized as social practice. In the understanding that we follow here, we are concerned, in discourses, with forms of 'institutional language use', with complexes of statements which make assertions about phenomena and which have more or less strongly formalized or formalizable claims to validity (on this and all further points in Chapter 3 below, see Keller 2005a).

Basic Terminology for Discourse Research[3]

Addressee/Audience: the person or persons to whom the discourse is directed or by whom it is received

Actor(s): individual or collective producers of statements; those who use specific rules and resources to (re)produce and transform a discourse by means of their practices

Discourse: a statement practice or totality of statement-events definable according to various criteria, which is investigated with regard to institutionally stabilized common structural patterns, practices, rules and resources for meaning-creation

Discourse Field, Discursive Field: the arena in which different discourses vie for the constitution or definition of a phenomenon

---

[3]This overview brings together the most important aspects of the terms; for greater detail on individual terms see also the explanations in the preceding chapters.

Discourse Formation (or Discursive Formation): characterization of a definable juxtaposition of discourse(s), actors, practices and *dispositifs* (e.g. modern reproductive medicine)

Discourse Fragment: Statement-event (utterance) in which discourses are more or less comprehensively actualized (e.g. a text); principal database for analysis

Discursive Practices: forms of statement production, which materialize, for example, in the form of texts (e.g. press releases, scientific articles, lectures)

Discourse Coalition: a group of actors whose statements can be attributed to the same discourse (e.g. through the use of the same 'storyline'); the amalgamation can, but does not have to take place consciously or strategically

Discourse Strategies: argument, rhetorical, practical strategies for the implementation of a discourse (e.g. 'black boxing', the setting up of unquestionable basic assumptions; protest events to gain the attention of the mass media; the taking of key positions in an institution)

Dispositif: the material and ideational infrastructure, i.e. the bundle of measures, regulations, artefacts, by means of which a discourse is (re)produced and achieves effects (e.g. laws, codes of behaviour, buildings, measuring devices)

Interpretative Repertoire:[4] the typified ensemble of interpretative components of which a discourse consists and which is more or less comprehensively actualized in individual utterances

Non-discursive Practices: forms of non-linguistic action (e.g. surveying, punishing, washing of hands) which are attributable to a discourse in particular cases (e.g. symbolic gestures, styles of clothing in religious discourses, but which can develop more or less independently of them and with their own dynamic)

Public Discourse: discourse with an orientation to a general audience in a public domain mediated by the mass media

Special Discourse: discourse within a partially public social domain, e.g. scientific contexts

Statement: the typifiable and typical core 'content' of a concrete utterance, or individual linguistic sequences contained within it, which may be reconstructed in a large number of disseminated utterances

Storyline: common thread of a discourse by means of which the different constituents of the interpretative repertoire are interconnected

(Continued)

---

[4]On Interpretative Repertoire see Potter and Wetherell (1987, 1998) and Chapter 5 (below).

(Continued)

Subject Position: 'places' that are contoured in the discourse and more or less strongly stabilized institutionally. These are places, or expectations and offers for possible speakers (speaker position; e.g. through preconditions for specific qualifications), or addressees (e.g. offered collective identity; models of the 'environmentally aware citizen')

Utterance/Statement-event: the concretely and individually documented singular linguistic materialization of a discourse or discourse fragment

Social science discourse analyses have a number of features in common with corpus linguistic discourse perspectives, as they are represented – between linguistic and historical research – in the approaches of linguistic discourse history or historical semantics (see Chapter 2.3). Thus, social science analyses of discourse also put together text corpora according to specific criteria, and analyse individual data as exemplary documentation of a discourse that consists of a finite but in reality unattainable number of utterances. The essential difference between linguistic and social science discourse research is to be found in the different research interests that are conditioned by the disciplines. The analysis of the linguistic or semiotic level of discourses is, for social science discourse research, only one component of their questions; in addition there is the analysis of the actors and processes which create, reproduce or challenge a discourse, the investigation of the situations and contexts of discourse production, and the question of the relationship of discourses, events and widely differing social practices – that is, levels 'external to' the text corpora. These are considered to be not only constraints on interpretations, but also independent fields of data elicitation. This is also true of ensuing questions such as those concerning social discourse relationships as definition and power relationships.

3.2 Questions

SKAD research is interested in statements, practices and dispositifs as manifestations of the structured processing of contingent social knowledge in discourses. It investigates processes of social construction and communication of symbolic orders in institutional fields of society, that is, social processes of the objectivization of knowledge, institutionalized orders of knowledge, social knowledge policies, their acquisition through social actors and the resultant reality effects. These orders of knowledge are manifest in linguistic, pictorial, practicable or material forms. For this sample, research questions can be formulated and processed in the context of concrete research undertakings with varying emphases (see text box).[5]

Questions in Social Science Discourse Research

- When does a specific discourse appear or disappear again?
- How, where and with what practices and resources is a discourse (re)produced?
- What linguistic and symbolic means and strategies are employed?
- What categories of phenomena are thus constituted and how?
- What formations of objects, utterance modalities, concepts and strategies does a discourse contain?
- What are the rules of formation and the processes and modalities of structuring?
- What are the decisive events in the development of a discourse, and how does it change over time?
- How is a discourse reflected in *dispositifs*?
- What actors occupy the positions of speakers using what resources, interests, and strategies?
- Who are the bearers, the addressees and the audience of the discourse?
- What modes of appropriation can be shown?
- What links does a discourse contain to other discourses?
- How can a discourse be related to more or less far-reaching temporal-spatial social contexts?
- What (power-)effects result from a discourse, and how do these react to fields of social practice and 'everyday representations'?
- What explanations are there for the features of a discourse?
- What phenomena are explained by Discourse Analysis?

Even if the empirical bases of social science Discourse Analysis are primarily texts, in a narrower sense a linguistic perspective is of secondary importance here. Questions of grammar, syntax, the use of specific rhetorical

---

[5]See Keller, Hirseland, Schneider and Viehöver (2010), Jaworski and Coupland (1999), Wetherell, Taylor and Yates (2001a,b). The questions are predominantly formulated in the singular; by analogy they could be represented for 'discourses'.

devices (metaphor, synecdoche, metonymy and so on) may be of interest in individual cases, for instance in order to explain the public resonance of a discourse. But so long as there is no presumption of a discourse specific relation to grammar, rhetorical elements, contents and speaker positions, these kinds of analytical instruments can largely be dispensed with for purposes of social science research. In what follows we shall put together and explain briefly some of the research questions we have introduced. In this we shall presuppose that one or more discourses or a discourse field, or an area of conflict, events or topics has been determined in advance, and that these are of research interest.

(1) Discourse Production

Discourse analyses are interested in determining in what institutional locations with what associated rules, and by means of what (collective) actors or events, discourses are disseminated in the form of concrete utterances. This is scarcely a matter of the search for a primary source, even if discourses themselves can claim such an origin, but of the shaping of the spatial situation and dissemination of a discourse that is essential for the particular question. The question of how many different discourses compete to constitute the phenomenon in a particular field must be explained both empirically *and* theoretically: the closer one comes to a discourse, the greater is the probable number of distinguishable 'sub-discourses'. What is crucial here, against the background of the question, is the level of abstraction that can be theoretically determined for the particular 'unit' of the discourse. This may be the institutional-organizational setting: we can speak rather easily of discourses, as Foucault did, in terms of scientific disciplines or specific religious denominations. In such cases speaker positions are clearly determined (by education, or qualification criteria). Public discourses, by contrast, have a more diffuse speaker-structure and different rules for the formulation of legitimate contents, and for these the types of function-logic of the mass media are of particular importance: it may be journalists, politicians, activists, scientists, businessmen and others who make their particular contributions. For this reason thematic reference acquires greater significance here. Ultimately, however, in the definition of every discourse, it is a matter of an analysis of situated statement practices with thematic references. For example, public protest discourses, in the area of environmental politics, may be traced back, in their thematic career, to the production of the first report in the mass media. The development of scientific, medical or therapeutic discourse is also capable of reconstruction. The questions of who, how, when and where are vital for understanding the discourses, their changes and effects, their structure, and so on. For instance, the analysis of public discourses on the problem of domestic waste in Germany demonstrates that even before the emergence of an environmental lobby this was already a topic of controversy and debate in the mass media, and that a variety of actors – government departments, trade associations, administrative bodies, local authorities and so on – were taking part in it (Keller 1998).

Discourses spread – indeed, 'are spread' – in more or less anonymized processes or practices of communication, supported by a variety of resources: discussion events, mass media (including films, reporting, news bulletins, features, talk shows, internet), self-help literature, law-texts and other regulations, textbooks and literature or professional therapeutic activity, processes of political negotiation, demonstrations from social movements and scientific debates. In the investigation of public discourses it is mostly reporting of the mass media, parliamentary events and the related activities of dedicated actors that are foregrounded. Max Weber, in his *Protestant Ethics*, which can be read as a study of discourse *avant la lettre*, analyzed religious self-help literature that contains guidelines for an 'orderly life'. Scientific and academic discourses are circulated in relevant journals, publications and meetings. SKAD research, using interview and text-based analysis of statement-events (utterances) and their contexts, in a thorough analysis, can take the form of an ethnographic inquiry and thus subject individual discourse events to a more detailed reconstruction (Keller 2003).

(2) The Constitution of Phenomena

Discourses produce and process complex relations of meaning that constitute reality in specific ways.[6] This has consequences for discourse research, and in particular for data collection: if objects are only created by discourse in their specific recognized form, then a discourse cannot be accessed simply on the basis of the object. A similar problem exists in talking about 'themes' as

---

[6]If we talk of a discourse 'doing' this or that, this is always an abbreviation for the relationship between structure, actors and practice in the sense of the 'duality of structure' mentioned above, or – to put it differently – for the interrelation between objectivized reality and the articulation practices of the actors.

identification markers and as the criterion for the unity of a discourse, since from a discourse-specific viewpoint themes can be treated very differently. The identification of data for an analysis of discourse is therefore a search-process in different directions that can always only orientate itself provision-ally to 'themes', reference phenomena, key terms and so on. For, one essential goal of discourse research is indeed to answer the question of what knowl-edge, what objects, relationships, properties, subject positions and so on are claimed by discourses to be 'real', by what means – such as meaning schemata, storylines, moral and ethical assessments – this takes place, and what different formation rules and resources underlie these processes. The practical linguistic construction of reality in discourses functions through difference-generation and sense or meaning concatenations. In other words: it also always contains implicit or explicit exclusions of other possibilities of meaning-making, the devaluation of competing positions, references to further supporting con-cepts, and so on. Discourse producers endeavour to give guidance as to modes of reading a discourse and they provide commenting or balancing text for this purpose. The question of the meaning structures which are built up in a discourse and which are stabilized or modified over time also leads to the analysis of the linguistic-rhetorical devices that are used, if it is a matter of analysing strategies and mechanisms for the creation of resonance in a social-cultural context: How are emotions aroused? What comparisons are made in order to convince? Does a discourse operate with specialist language, alienat-ing abstraction devices, or polemic depictions? And in this context, to what extent is it a matter of the particular features of a specific discourse? For exam-ple, in general, specialist discourses need to be translated into other linguistic games and narrative forms if they are intended to attract public awareness and produce a social effect. In the public debate about climate change, for example, the use of the greenhouse-metaphor advanced the broad reception of a specific discourse on climate (Viehöver 2010).

(3) *Dispositifs*, (Power-) Effects, Practices

Discourses exist as use of language in historically and institutionally situated statement-events (utterances) and in the form of *dispositifs*. Together with the constitution of phenomena that takes place through them there arise – if in a general sense they demonstrate power-effects – 'inner-worldly' objectifica-tions in the form of material objects (buildings, technologies, etc.), practices (such as the execution of punishments, or refuse disposal) and elements in the form of texts (such as the adoption of laws, formalized action guidelines and so on). In the form of *dispositifs* discourses are institutionalized, materialized, reproduced and thereby exert 'power-effects' (Jürgen Link). The relationship of the individual utterance to general discourse structure is borne – in the sense of Giddens' theory of structurization – by temporo-spatial materializations. It was Michel Foucault who repeatedly drew attention to the interplay and affinities of discourses, practices and artefacts, starting with relevant legal texts, passing by the organization of institutional processing routines, and extending to the architectural totality of a building, such as a prison complex. At the same time he stressed the possibility and the occurrence of relatively independent and self-dynamic developments of discourse and practice. For this reason the levels of the development of practices, artefacts and discourses should initially be dealt with separately; it is a question of theoretical and empirical fantasy, whether and how it is possible to reconstruct the fact that discourses produce or organize relevant relationships.[7]

(4) Subject Positions and Actors

Subject positions play an important role in discourses in a variety of ways (Keller, Schneider and Viehöver 2012). In the first instance it is a matter of the speaker positions available for social actors in the discourse and their regulation. For example, it is only after completion of specific levels of qualifications that a speaker is allowed to take part in scientific discourses; in public discourse an achieved status of prominence or a position as spokesperson for an association can fulfil similar functions. Speaker positions such as these can then be taken up by a variety of individual actors ('role-players'). Even when a discourse is made up of scattered statement-events – for example a discourse on environmental politics in the context of local evening events at different places in the country – instances of discourse-internal structuring and hierarchy formation may still be detected, that is to say, in the sense of the prominence of, or public respect for, particular determinable actors. Power resources such as money, knowledge and symbolic, economic social or cultural capital play an important role in understanding the spread of discourses, the interplay of the participating actors and their external effects. Such power resources do not necessarily have (only) a discourse-internal

---

[7]See the works of Foucault cited in Chapter 2.6.

origin; they are constituted in the interplay between discourses, speakers and audience. Symbolic capital, for example, can be developed with a strategic intention. But whether or not this functions depends on the addressees or the audience. Discourses are directed to potential addressees and configure these in a specific way. Waldschmidt (1996), for instance, demonstrates how experts' counselling discourse on human genetics defines its clients as subjects with specific qualities and needs. In discourse theory and research, Laclau and Mouffe in particular, and works following their ideas, have directed their attention to these kinds of 'identity markers' in the form of difference-formations in political discourses – for example, following the pattern of a positive 'we' that includes the addressees, as opposed to a negative 'the others' (see Shapter 2.6 above).

(5) Discourses and Everyday Representations

Social science discourse research can finally also consider the extent to which discourses are manifest in everyday life-world communication processes and practices. For example in family disputes about the just division of housework we find particles of feminist equality-discourse; discussions of the right way to bring up children contain elements from natural science and pedagogic discourses that are circulating through different channels of dissemination in the mass media; 'pub talk' caricatures neoliberal economic discourses, and so on. Consequently, discourse-oriented perspectives can direct our attention to the ways in which everyday knowledge, everyday representations or 'subjective worlds of meaning' are partly shaped by processes of collective knowledge and dissemination through the (mass) media. However, everyday subjects in their life-practice cannot be understood as simple mouthpieces for pre-formed components. They behave, rather, as more or less individual, creatively interpreting 'meaning-tinkers' (Hitzler 1994) in the social context of very different and heterogeneous discursive fields and contests.[8] Of course the pursuit of such questions, if it wishes to avoid the (re)production of over-hasty stereotypes, will presuppose the knowledge and analysis of relevant discourses.

---

[8]Taking the example of environmental discussion and everyday ecological practice, see Poferl (2004). The afore-mentioned individual treatment of discourses is an important theme in Cultural Studies (see Chapter 2.6 above). On the 'Knowledge of People' on bioethical questions, see Waldschmidt, Klein and Korte (2009).

3.3 General Foundations

The catalogue of questions introduced above already suggests that discourse research sets out as 'multi-methodological' and correlates a variety of data and methods – and for particular questions it also uses quantitative procedures. The choice of the concrete procedures for data collection and analysis must take place in accordance with the basic theoretical assumptions about discourse and the particular research interests. The scarcity of resource provision, that is to say, the shortage of staff, time and money, but also – in many cases – the (im)possibility of access to data impose constraints on the research process.[9]

Only in very exceptional cases is it possible to process the spectrum of the specified questions and other possible questions within the context of a single research project. For this reason we shall not present here any 'standard model' of Discourse Analysis. In the proposals that follow it is rather a matter of a general orientation which sets out the most important steps or stages in empirical discourse research and demonstrates possible options for their design.[10] Concrete examples of Discourse Analysis, depending on their capacity, deal with a specific focus. At the centre of the procedure are data predominantly in textual form, i.e. 'natural' statement-events or reports of these. As 'Interpretative Analytics' (Dreyfus and Rabinow 1982; Keller 2005b) social science Discourse Analysis combines a precise analytical dissection of statement-events with stages of a hermeneutically reflected and controlled interpretation. The analysis of the language used is directed primarily to the content that is thereby constructed, i.e. the order of knowledge of worldly phenomena that is thus outlined; linguistic questions in the narrower sense are excluded, so long as they do not have any specific reference to the social structuring or reception of the content, and therefore do not appear to be relevant from a social science perspective.

---

[9]By means of the partially digitized, cheap and easy availability of some types of document (such as newspaper texts from particular publishers, for particular periods of time) many questions now are easy to handle. Documents that are difficult to access – such as historical texts, 'secret' reports, and so on – require more elaborate research in archives.

[10]Guilhaumou (2010) emphasizes that it is indeed only the non-standardization and openness of the modes of operation in Discourse Analysis that gives scope for creativity and makes possible surprising new discoveries.

3.3.1 Discourse Research is Interpretative Work

Discourse Analysis is always and inevitably a process of hermeneutic textual interpretation (Keller 2005b). The dispute concerning methods of discourse research was initially coloured by structuralist attacks against all hermeneutics and an explicitly linked claim to superiority of a standardized analytical procedure of primarily linguistic or lexicometric origin, contrasting with the 'uncontrolled' hermeneutic-interpretative approaches. In this respect it reproduced a widespread academic power struggle in France in the 1960s (see Chapter 2). In particular the French *analyse du discours* advanced the claim that the subjective factor of the researcher should be eliminated by means of 'automatized', quantifying, computer-assisted methods of analysis, and a genuinely scientific and objective form of text analysis should then be established (Williams 1999; Guilhaumou 2010). It was not by chance, however, that this programme, with its radical character, is now regarded as having failed; and it is equally not a coincidence that Dreyfus and Rabinow (1982) characterized Foucault's approach as 'interpretative analytics', and by the use of this term have thus brought together interpretative and analytical procedures. At a very early stage Paul Ricœur pointed out that analyses of discourse always operate within the 'paradigm of text-interpretation' (Ricœur 1974, 1977, 1981). They are essentially hermeneutic approaches, for which the world represents 'the ensemble of references opened up by the texts' (Ricœur 1981: 197). They even imply textual *interpretations* when they are concentrating on formal structures, objects or practices. The above-mentioned *analyse du discours* has meanwhile also recognized the boundaries of 'automatic' Discourse Analysis and now regards itself – according to the reception of ethnomethodological approaches – as a fully 'interpretative discipline' (Guilhaumou 2010).

To speak of hermeneutics or interpretation does not mean, in the context of Discourse Analysis, the search for the subjective and possibly concealed intentions of the author of a text or his 'class attitude'. Nor is it a matter of attributing to a particular statement-event a 'true', 'absolute' or 'objective' meaning. More recent social science hermeneutics is concerned, rather, with the possibilities of methodical control of interpretative processes, and it is precisely in this respect that it is relevant to discourse research.[11] Certainly – as Ricœur

---

[11]Umberto Eco (1991), using the example of an invitation to a conference sent to him by Jacques Derrida, draws the reader's attention to the fact that one can certainly invoke infinite readings of texts, but that fortunately we normally operate within certain conventionalized interpretative pathways.

points out – there are no fixed rules and known 'recipes' with a guarantee of success for the development of 'convincing' interpretation hypotheses. It is rather that abductive conclusions, that it is to say ideas, thoughts or flashes of insight that derive from dealing with the relevant data material, play an important role (Reichertz 2009). Competing readings and alternative modes of procedure are always possible and – within certain limits and with good reasons – may be considered 'accountable'. In this, as Ricœur emphasized – there is also the possibility of generating more appropriate or convincing interpretations.

However, if sociology wishes to be an empirical science and not 'fiction' or reportage, the requirement for principled disclosure and clarity in the relevant stages of an interpretation must be met. This in turn makes essential a certain degree of methodological system in the procedure. This is true irrespective of the level – in the consciousness or knowledge of the actors, in documents and so on – at which the particular symbolic order is fixed: reality is always both a matter of 'achievement through consciousness' and a symbolic-interactive social construct (Luckmann 1999). Since Discourse Analysis is concerned above all with text analysis, it makes sense to use the sociology of knowledge type of reconstructive hermeneutics. The following proposals may be understood in that way:[12]

> 'The methodology of qualitative social research, with its particular data collection and data analysis procedures, therefore aims at systematizing and controlling the scientific reconstruction of constructions of reality. Here qualitative methods are to be understood less as prescriptions than as sensitizations to typical problems of the research process – such as adequacy, coherence, reliability, validity and checkability' (Hitzler and Honer 2002: 758).[13]

In social science hermeneutics, in recent decades, different approaches have been developed within methodologically controlled interpretative text analysis. These include the Documentary Method of Interpretation, Objective Hermeneutics, forms of Frame Analysis and Analysis of Interpretative Schemes, applications of Grounded Theory, approaches to Conversation

---

[12]Under the umbrella of social science hermeneutics, a variety of procedures in qualitative social research are to be found, all of which aim at methodologically controlled reconstruction of sense and meaning (Hitzler and Honer 1997).

[13]I have slightly modified this quotation: in the original the topic is 'everyday reconstructions of reality'.

Analysis, and others.[14] Despite important differences between the above-mentioned concepts and methods of analysis, they are united by their concern for a self-reflective stance that takes account of the interpretative achievements of social researchers and forms and uses them in a methodologically clear fashion, in order to provide good reasons for the particular range of interpretations. In the process, of course, formal and context-dependent features of text are also borne in mind in the reconstruction process.

3.3.2 The Adaptation of Qualitative Methods

The Sociology of Knowledge Approach to discourse research views texts, practices or artefacts not as products of 'subjective' or 'objective' case-structures, but as material manifestations of social orders of knowledge. They are thus the most important basis for a sociology of knowledge reconstruction of the production, stabilization and change of *collective* stocks of knowledge. Discourse as an object requires a specific adaptation of the available methods of qualitative social research and text analysis:

– discourse research is interested in statements, practices and *dispositifs* as manifestations of the structured processing of controversial social knowledge. Its constituents can be worked out by means of various methods of reconstruction; it is possible to complement qualitative procedures with quantified data. Discourse research is *not* concerned with the reconstruction of subjective meaning attributions or individuals' stocks of knowledge, with the analysis of 'small life-worlds' or the ethnographic exploration of 'strange worlds around the corner'. Neither is it concerned with 'subjective' case-structures or biographical narrative, nor with 'objective case-structures of interactive relationships, the formation of identities and so on.
– A further difference between discourse analyses and other approaches in interpretative social research is to be found in the adoption of supra-textual cross-references in the form of rules and resources, i.e. structures in statement-production. Individual utterances do not amount to individual 'types' (as in

---

[14]Hitzler and Honer (1997), Soeffner and Hitzler (1994), Soeffner (1979,1989, 2004) Hitzler (2000), Hitzler, Reichertz and Schröer (1999a), Bohnsack (1999), Flick (2009), Flick, Kardorff and Steinke (2004).

---

biographical research); mostly they do not give a complete representation of only a single discourse.

– Discourses always exist in an inter-discursive context and relationship to historically diachronic and synchronic discourse formations. They must be successively reconstructed from individual utterances. This aggregation of particular results of analysis to general statements about 'the discourse' marks the central difference from most qualitative approaches, which work on the basis of a single consistent and self-contained meaning and case structure for each text (normally an interview). This means that they view a text as a complete document precisely for a single case. What is typical of the Discourse Analysis perspective on natural text-types is indeed the simultaneous heterogeneous and partial representation of discourse-specific elements; for this reason the results of the analysis of individual texts must be subjected to a process of interrelation.

– Social science discourse analyses are confronted with the problem of large quantities of text. Qualitative data analysis procedures are used mostly for small quantities of text and are only partially suited to the large text corpora of discourse research. For this reason they cannot simply be taken over, but have to be adapted to the research interests of Discourse Analysis. Analyses are set up as both qualitatively reconstructive and also (occasionally) quantitatively measuring. Quantitative approaches initially reconstruct, using individual texts, categories that become elements of content-oriented coding devices applicable to larger quantities of texts.[15] Qualitative approaches employ different strategies of corpus reduction such as the selection of key points, key texts or the theory-driven reduction of material, in order to achieve a manageable amount of text (see Chapter 4.2.3). In research practice work on the text – as elsewhere in qualitative social research – focuses on the reconstruction of typical or typifiable structural elements which can be seen in a variety of ways – as cognitive, classificatory or narrative structures, as meaning patterns, topoi and so on – and which underlie, as meaning-creating patterns, the discourses that are being studied.

---

[15]On this, see the works cited in Chapter 2.5 by Gamson and others, and the subsequent analyses by Ferree, Gamson, Gerhards, and Rucht (2002) or Brand, Eder and Poferl (1997). This procedure differs substantially from linguistic corpus-based discourse analyses (Chapter 2.3). On the difference between content analysis and Discourse Analysis that sometimes disappears in research practice, see Diaz-Bone and Schneider (2010).

3.3.3 Problems of Demarcation and Validity

Discourse research relies predominantly on natural data, that is to say, oral, written, audiovisual statement-events, observable practices, more rarely also material objects from the field of investigation. In addition, new data are generated through interviews or focus groups, and also by means of focused ethnography (Knoblauch 2005a, 2001), and so on. What scope the empirical material should have, in order to be able to make valid statements about the specific discourse(s) that is/are of interest, depends essentially on the question being pursued or else must be justified with reference to that. In general terms the assembled material may be observed from two points of view. On the one hand it serves as information about the field (the aspect of knowledge or information). On the other hand, it works as a document for the reconstruction of discourses, their material and linguistic resources and their contents. In this respect the value of the analysed documents must be justified with regard to the discourse(s). The whole of the assembled material functions as a discourse-internal or discourse-external context for the individual data that are investigated in detail. How the work on the individual text is carried out, whether, for instance, sequence-analytical procedures, the method of documentary interpretation, or procedures of category-formation are used, and how they are linked to descriptions of formal structures or external context data: these cannot be determined *ex cathedra*. Even when there is no royal road in Discourse Analysis, the decisions taken must still be justified and explained. As a basis one may distinguish here between 'problems of demarcation' and questions of 'establishing validity':

- We may describe as demarcation problems various situations of decision that arise in the planning and execution of empirical investigations. These include the delimitation of the times and objects of an investigation, questions of the delimitation and context of the material to be analysed, and the problem of the attribution of documents/practices or individual contents to discourses.
- The different steps of data interpretation must also be justified in respect of the claims to validity of an investigation. In detail this is a question of the decision between different procedures in the detailed analysis, of the interrelating of heterogeneous databases or the triangulation of different methodological approaches, the relation of individual documents to discourses, the problem of reaching saturation in the analytical process – when has everything important been fulfilled? – and finally it is a matter of the process of

theoretical abstraction and interpretation, that is of the formulation of statements about the whole discourse and the meaning of the results (Reichertz and Schröer 1994; Keller 2005a; Flick 2009: 381ff).

3.3.4 More than Text Analysis

Hitherto – irrespective of any Discourse Analysis paradigm that is being considered – discourse research has investigated almost exclusively texts: books, laws, court judgments, leaflets, information brochures, articles in newspapers and periodicals, interviews, transcripts of conversations and so on. This concentration on data fixed in writing is an understandable and justified consequence of the main questions in discourse research. In addition analyses of discourse for purposes of information and interpretation have naturally drawn upon different forms of contextual knowledge and accessible materials concerning the research field – secondary scientific literature, available general knowledge, and so on – in order to deal with their questions. However, the above-mentioned concentration on texts, which is true of all qualitative research, is in many respects in need of supplementation and extension:

- In view of the enormous significance of audiovisual media formats and contents (television, film, photography, comics, advertising) discourse analyses will in future have to focus more strongly on the analysis and interpretation of these kinds of data. In this context links to Cultural Studies may be helpful.
- Another extension of Discourse Analysis perspectives requires the inclusion of non-textual components of *dispositifs* (artefacts such as buildings, machines, technologies), and also the practical contexts that discourses encounter. For sociology, much more than in the historical sciences, there arises the possibility of recording and analyzing the production and reception of discourses '*in actu*'. For this it can make use of various methods of observation and reporting, different forms of recording conversations and related analytical strategies. This makes it easier to avoid wrong or shorthand 'idealistic' conclusions about a simplified relationship between 'discourse' and 'practice'. In the sense of triangulation (Flick 2009: 443ff) it is then a question of correlating different methodological perspectives on the particular domain. In methodological terms connections can be made here to the social science tradition of comprehensive case studies.

FOUR

Doing Discourse Research

4.1 Getting started

The term 'discourse' refers to a construct of social researchers. This assumes hypothetically that a relation, rule or structure underlies specific empirical data, which primarily exist and are documented as events (utterances) that are disseminated in time and place. This kind of assumption *must* be used as the search hypothesis for the compilation of a data corpus. The concrete character of the data corpus, that is, its scope and its components, is oriented towards the goals of the investigation. It may consist of recorded oral speech, a variety of written texts, audio-visual materials, observation reports and even artefacts. Under the perspective of 'discourse' it is a question of investigating the social mechanisms and rules for the production and structuring of orders of knowledge. It is therefore possible that particular data which are collected, for example, according to coarse thematic markers, cannot be reconstructed as parts of the discourse being studied, and therefore have to be excluded from the data corpus in the course of the research process. In this sense an analysis of discourse may also fail if insufficient attention is paid to the 'coherence' of the basic data. The methodological approaches that are followed in the concrete analysis must be decided in relation to the specific question, the data selection used and the planned empirical or analytical depth of an investigation. For example, a study that involves large expanses of history will require different methods compared to a synchronic preoccupation with current discourse events; the procedure used in the analysis of large text documents (e.g. textbooks) needs a different methodology than the analysis of pamphlets, printed texts (e.g. from newspapers), discussion reports or films. Discourse research operates across the whole spectrum of broad historical processes of knowledge construction and communication, the concentration on concrete policy-processes, the reconstructive qualitative and (now) computer-supported analysis of single texts, oriented according to parameters of interpretative social research, or the more or less standardized content-analysis coding of larger text corpora – to name only a few variants. It is directed, first and foremost, at the analysis of the interplay of statement-production, the formal appearance and structured content of statements with their situational, institutional, organizational and social-historical context, and a variety of social practices.

For orientation in respect of the following suggested methodological stages and with reference to the traditions of qualitative social research, see Flick's comprehensive introduction (Flick 2009); on object-related theory-formation (Grounded Theory) see Strauss (1991), Strauss and Corbin (1998); on concepts and methods of Social Science Hermeneutics, see the contributions in Hitzler and Honer (1997). For a fuller consideration of the discourse perspective see the contributions in Keller, Hirseland, Schneider and Viehöver (2010, 2011).

The questions of the moment in time or the social/institutional level where we may speak of a discourse cannot be formulated independently of the particular research interests. The discursive unity or coherence of texts may fade away according to the degree to which the context in which they are spoken or written is no longer that of a specialist discourse, but a more general public domain or arena. Many textual documents in public discourses, such as expert reports in the policy-process, and books or background stories in the media, are composed of a number of specialist discourses. For example, in a textbook, the introduction may be a piece of reformist discourse, the factual chapter may be a hard-core scientific discourse, and the conclusions a social science discourse. The multiple types of reality are matched not only by the diversity of discourses and practices in which manifold realities are socially constructed, but also by the multiplicity of discourse-analysis approaches that decode them. In the research process, discourse researchers must arrive at a number of general decisions and solve problems that do not represent any special feature of Discourse Analysis. These may be summarized in various stages in the analysis (see below text box).[1] In addition to the choice of topic, the formulation of research questions, the development of a theoretical and conceptual base, and the discussions and selection of related methodological applications, it is also possible to distinguish phases in the analysis of relevant scientific literature, the final interpretation and the formulation of results. In general the individual phases, particularly the analysis of the literature, and the collection and analysis of data, are rarely implemented in strict linear succession. More frequently there are reciprocating movements between the different steps in the research process. The very research question itself is also clarified, modified and sometimes even abandoned in favour of a new perspective that has arisen.

From the perspective of research practice the following methodological steps should, basically, be adhered to: Discourse Analysis begins by determining the field(s) of knowledge or discourse to be investigated. This can take place very crudely in terms of a thematic tag (such as 'abortion'), an institutional setting (e.g. the general public arena), or such different special arenas as politics, law or science, or arenas related to the actors (such as the discourse of 'the Greens'). Alternatively this may happen in terms of different combinations of these criteria. A following step consists of a first, provisional formulation of the research questions (see Chapter 3.2) related to the object of the investigation, and these may be modified in the course of the investigation. This is followed by the appropriate definition of the elements of the investigation, its conceptualization in terms of discourse theory, and the selection of suitable processes of data collection and analysis. At the beginning of the practical part of the research process there is initially a collection of accessible information about the research object. This is done through the reception of appropriate scientific and non-scientific literature, and possibly also in the context of exploratory interviews with experts in the field. Following this a start is made, in this phase, with the collection of data, i.e. the assembly of the data corpus. The analysis of data can begin, even if a corpus is not yet considered to be 'concluded'. In the sense of qualitative social research it may be absolutely necessary to expand the corpus when required. Phases of detailed, fine analysis of individual data now alternate with phases of hypothesis-formation, theoretical consolidation and the presentation of

---

[1]See also Flick (2009: 87ff).

interim results, until ultimately the investigation may be seen as 'finished'. In the course of the different steps in the analysis it is vital to pay constant attention to the 'fit' between question, methodological implementation and the basic data material. The process of reconstruction is concluded with a summarizing interpretation and the processing of the results.

Conceptual stages in the research process

- What are the objects, domains and questions of the investigation?
- What are the basic theoretical assumptions and hypotheses that relate to these?
- How can an appropriate conceptual structuring be undertaken?
- What would a matching methodological implementation look like?
- What resources for processing are available?
- How can the data corpus be put together?
- What analytical procedures should be used?
- What role is played by the social, historical or situational context? In what form can these contexts be incorporated in the investigation or the interpretation of data?
- How can generalizable statements be made about the object of investigation, i.e. The discourse(s) under investigation?
- When is the analysis concluded and what are the results?
- How are the results presented, and what do they yield?

4.2 The Exploration of the Field of Investigation

It is essential, before and during data collection, to inform oneself from various sources (e.g. scholarly books and popular literature, exploratory expert interviews, more probing interviews with key actors in the course of research), about the intended field, the object of investigation in general, and in particular about the state of the scholarly debate concerning the intended questions. This will make it possible to give a very precise although preliminary account of the area of concern of the research. These tasks are normally carried out in the preparatory stage of an investigation. In this early phase, and subsequently in parallel to the data collection, knowledge of the field of investigation is further expanded by means of a study of the relevant literature. The information thus obtained will help to make more precise the questions to be pursued and the formation of an adequate database. This is not only a matter of the basic question as to the nature and the processing of the data, but also, in terms of research practice, of the possibilities of access to such data, for example in existing databases, libraries and archives, the internet and actor-related collections of material.

The knowledge of a field or arena of discourse that is made available by observers or protagonists may, in every sense, be used to develop targeted and comprehensive strategies for the procurement of the researcher's own data. The special potential of exploratory interviews lies in the comparatively rapid access to the (perhaps contradictory) assessments of important events, positions, arenas, processes, practices and actors in the field of investigation. These may then be used as bases for the compilation of data – not, of course, in a naïve or credulous manner, but after due critical reflection. Similarly, direct (participant) observation of relevant discursive settings (e.g. different kinds of informative or discussion events) can provide first impressions of important elements of the structure of a field of discourse. In general terms the researcher should avoid simply adopting without reflection the interpretations of the object of investigation that are suggested in the available literature, in interviews and other 'field encounters' as a guide for his/her own further research procedure.

4.3 Selection of Data

4.3.1 Data Formats

For the analysis of discourse, various data formats need to be considered. We may distinguish between data in textual form (books, legal texts, instructions, newspaper articles, reports of interviews and discussions and so on), audio-visual data (pictures, films, music), objectifications (e.g. church buildings, chalices, robes) and observable social practices (such as demonstrations, symbolic gestures). The data to be collected must match the questions being investigated: in order to investigate the topic-related discourse of a social movement, it is sensible to rely initially on documents from the context of the movement itself, and not on press reports or television commentaries and the like (the analysis of which may, however, be useful to understand the discourse of the movement itself or its public resonance). If one wishes to reconstruct specific decisions about content or its representation it is helpful to use different versions of texts and in some cases to clarify them through interviews.

In general, discourse analyses do not relate to a single document or a small number of individual documents of the same type; rather, they bring together a larger corpus of documents. The most important access is provided by all kinds of 'natural' documents in linguistic form, from pamphlets to newspaper articles, parliamentary speeches, legal texts, advertisements, advisory literature, internet texts, recordings of interviews, and expert reports. The extent to which a document refers to one – or several – discourses is a question to be clarified by empirical research. Pamphlets, for example, are certainly to a large extent the expression of a specific discourse; newspapers, articles or books may intertwine different discourses with each other in more or less complex ways, or put them in opposition to one another. Within documents of this sort, statements or networks of statements form the basic components of the discourses.

Audio-visual data (such as pictures, television broadcasts, films, advertising trailers, cartoons) play an important role in the social circulation of meaning. Hitherto they have had only a marginal position in discourse research: this is related, on the one hand, to the available technical possibilities for the reproduction of such complex data, and, on the other hand, to the costs (e.g. time, manpower) involved in the analysis. Discourse Analysis is faced here with the particular problem of how it can proceed from the laborious analysis of individual documents to discourse structures.

Similarly, the investigation of artefacts has so far not played a significant role in discourse research. As data they can be described in their meaning and functioning and can be accessed through field observation and the application of specialized knowledge (e.g. on the functioning of particular machines).

In the past, most analyses of discourse were only indirectly concerned with social practices. This may partly be justified by the relevant disciplinary embedding, particularly in historical contexts. For social science analyses of discourse, however, there is a basic possibility of full 'in actu' observation of discursive practices and modes of the reception of discourses in fields of social practice ('doing discourse'). The collection of these kinds of data may be achieved through observer participation and recorded in ethnographic descriptions

4.3.2 Corpus Building

Since textual data constitute the main basis of discourse analyses, the relevant options for compiling data corpora will now be explained in more detail.[2] Textual data can be used in discourse analyses in various ways. If they are used as a source of information about the field of investigation, it is appropriate to put together as many different documents, and of as many different types, as possible. If it is then a question, in the narrower sense, of reconstructing discourse structures through detailed analysis, it will be necessary to make stronger demands of consistency on the data. The different options can best be demonstrated with a few examples of social science Discourse Analysis:[3]

In his comparative investigation of political discussions on acid rain in Great Britain and the Netherlands, Hajer (1995) – in addition to numerous interviews with experts – used the most important scientific and political documents from particular decision processes, and reconstructed from them the basic argument structures of the discourses in question. To the fore is the interplay between political and scientific actors with their respective positions in the processes of discussion and decision-making

Schneider (1999) investigated the process of parliamentary discussion of the definition of brain death and questions of organ transplantation in the context of the German Transplantation Law of 1997, using the relevant protocols of parliamentary debates, expert opinions and legislation from the years 1995–1997. He took account of commentaries and appeals from various associations as well as articles from the printed media.

Keller (1998), in his investigation of processes of public discussion concerning the 'correct' policy for household waste disposal, referred to a systematic sample of text from the printed media (news, reports, commentaries), covering

---

[2]The following explanations are also valid, by analogy, for audio-visual data.

[3]Apart from social sciences' possibility of direct field research, interviewing and observation (which, by the way, is not given in every case of concern), there is, in terms of textual data, no basic difference from historical or linguistic corpus building. For further possibilities see Keller, Hirseland, Schneider and Viehöver (2010).

the spectrum of 'serious' newspapers for the years 1970 – 1995 in France and Germany, the countries under investigation. In addition, use was made of interviews with and documents from actors in the debates – from the fields of politics, business, social movements, administration and science. Similarly constructed media samples also formed the basis of the discourse analyses by Ferree, Gamson, Gerhards and Rucht (2002) concerning public debates on abortion, those of Viehöver (2010) on global climate change or, using relevant fan magazines, those of Diaz-Bone (2008) on the 'heavy metal' and 'techno' music styles.

Waldschmidt (1996), in her discussion of expert discourses on genetic counselling in the years 1945–1990, concentrates on key texts in this discussion. For the selection of these key texts, relevant criteria were used (such as circulation, frequency of citation, expert evaluations). Maasen (1998), in her historical study on the 'Genealogy of Immorality', proceeded in similar fashion. Sarasin (2001), in his investigation of the social discourses on hygiene from the eighteenth – twentieth centuries, refers to a sample of relevant literature from experts and advisers.

Gottweis (1998) used expert interviews and central archive documents covering a decade of the scientific and policy fields of genetic engineering in order to account for the politics of 'governing molecules' in the US and in Europe. Litfin (1994) started from the Montreal Protocol and followed discursive engagements of scientific, political and social movement actors in order to account for the unfolding of ozone regulation policies.

The composition of the data is mostly achieved using a range of databases, for example press archives and search facilities, libraries and special archives. Meanwhile, in the area of the print media in particular, texts on CD-ROM or on the internet have also become available. Compared to the 'originals' there may be changes in the data here, with the result that original contexts and publication formats are lost – and with them certain pieces of important information that may be significant. This is particularly true of documents which are made available via the world wide web but which were not originally designed for it, in contrast to online editions of periodicals or the websites of associations, and so on.

The construction of – according to the case in question – more or less comprehensive corpora requires resources in terms of time, (wo)manpower and finance. It requires permanent monitoring and questioning with regard to its intended composition and the necessary degree of completeness. This includes, for example, checking the extent to which the selected resources – such as press-cutting agencies or archives – are themselves selective in their operation, i.e. only document specific extracts about or from texts that must then be supplemented from other sources. This also includes an ongoing check of whether the required documents arrive and whether they are truly suitable for the question at issue. In many cases corpus formation must already direct itself to the ideas of *theoretical sampling* (Strauss and Corbin 1998; Corbin and Strauss 2007; Strauss 1987; Glaser and Strauss 1967). This term, taken from *Grounded Theory*, indicates that not only the analysis but also the compilation of the data must already be carried out according to theory-driven or reflected criteria.[4] The selection of key texts already requires intensive work in the particular field and the available literature, in order to be able to define criteria for this kind of key role and to direct subsequent text selection in accordance with these. The compilation of texts from the printed media, which can initially take place according to key words in the title, and so on, also requires – if its appropriateness is to be assessed – an orientation in terms of criteria for exclusion, that is to say, justified indicators for deciding which texts ultimately belong in a sample and which should not be included. The form in which the data are or should be made available – whether as transcripts or text-documents, as originals or in digitized form – depends on such factors as whether the use of any software for qualitative analysis is to be used (Diaz-Bone and Schneider 2010).[5] In most cases, however, there is some 'manual processing' by means of reading, marking, sorting and so on, that is not undertaken on the computer screen but in the text itself.

---

[4]Grounded Theory, i.e. object-related theory-formation, is a research approach in qualitative social research, developed by Anselm Strauss and Barney Glaser. It aims at making possible theoretically rich reconstructions of (inter)action processes – such as supervisory visits in hospitals. For this Glaser and Strauss (1967) presented different concepts which can be transferred to discourse research, if they are slightly modified for the purposes of the latter (Strauss and Corbin 1998; Strauss 1987; Glaser 1978). The embedding of discourse perspectives into Grounded Theory was undertaken by Clarke (2005).

[5]AtlasTi and MaxQDA are widely-used programs. In France, one of the programs used is PROSPERO.

Key Questions in Data Collection (Corpus Building)

- What data fit the question being investigated? What time intervals and social-spatial units should be collected?
- Are these data available in the intended object-area?
- What range of data can be collected within the framework of the available resources and processed with the intended form of data analysis?
- Through what sources can these data be accessed?
- Are these sources selective? According to what criteria do they match their pre-selection? Is any complementation or correction in the data selection needed?
- Are the collected data really suited to the question, for example in respect of the relevant time-horizon, thematic scope and specificity, or recording of the actors?
- Are subsequent collections necessary?
- When does the scope of the data correspond to the research requirements, i.e. when is the data collection at an end? How can this be justified?

4.3.3 The Selection of Data for Detailed Analysis

With regard to the analysis of data, we must distinguish whether they are to provide information – for example, about important events and actors – or whether they underlie the reconstruction of a particular discourse structure. Neither is excluded, but they do require different approaches to texts and should therefore be kept apart in terms of procedure. In the first case the analytical technique consists of simple reading and 'evaluation' of the information that seems to be of importance (e.g. pointers as to central actors who are then contacted); in addition, if possible, all the documents in the corpus should be utilized. In the second case, specific, controlled analytical and interpretative techniques are necessary, at least in cases where more should be achieved than a simple 're-telling' of discourse processes. The full articulation of a discourse in one single document is a rather improbable case. For this reason discourse analyses must rely on detailed analyses of a larger or smaller quantity of individual statement-events. The fine analysis of these statement-events is an interpretative act that depends on the competences of the researcher. It is demanding of resources, and as a rule cannot include all the data in the corpus. On the contrary, it must arrive at a systematically reflected and justified selection of texts or textual extracts within the corpus, i.e. it must subject the data corpus to further restrictions, and particularly in respect of the need to produce statements about the discourse as a whole.[6] Here attention should be paid to ensuring a certain degree of breadth but also comparability in the data selected from the corpus, to avoid or at least reduce the problem of an unintended comparison of 'apples' and 'pears' within the data: a pamphlet cannot be placed immediately alongside an expert opinion; a news bulletin or a commentary differ considerably from a multi-page piece of journalistic reportage. For this step of controlled consolidation of the data material to be analyzed, a number of criteria are available. Among these is the reflected orientation towards key texts, key passages, actors and events, the value of which can be worked out from the data material itself. Further selection criteria would include covering the spectrum of meanings from the relevant actors or the mass media.[7]

Guidelines for the Selection of Data for Detailed Analysis

To what extent should it be assumed that a selected document provides answers/results relevant to the question being investigated?

Is it a matter of typical, exemplary utterances, key texts, passages, actors and events?

Does it include the institutional fields, actors, positions and modes of articulation that may be identifiable as relevant?

Is the research goal more oriented to breadth or depth of reconstruction? With reference to this, how is a document to be located?

How do the selected data fit each other and the targeted discourse or discursive field?

(Continued)

---

[6]Of course, this is conversely also true of quantitative methods, such as content analysis: there large corpora can indeed be analyzed, but only with regard to a small number of features.

[7]See Keller, Hirseland, Schneider and Viehöver (2010), and also Flick (2009: 114ff).

- – The interchange between individual fine analyses and further data selection may take place according to the principles of theoretical sampling, minimal and maximal contrast

- – The original questions may change in the course of the fine analysis, i.e. as a result of confrontation with the data, and may require a modification in the strategies for further data selection

---

The selection of data for fine analysis is an open and criteria-driven search process, not intended to lead to the swift formation of a definitive partial corpus within the overall corpus. Instead it traverses and records successively the breadth of the entire data material. Depending upon the requirements of individual detailed analyses new criteria may emerge for the selection of further data. For these successive and interrelated stages of selection an orientation towards Grounded Theory is appropriate (e.g. Strauss and Corbin 1998, Strauss 1987). In the first instance Theoretical Sampling and the Principles of Minimal or Maximal Contrast play an important role here. It is a matter of justifying the choice of documents to be used for the fine analysis from the research process itself: the researcher begins with a document that seems to be 'significant' and then looks within the data corpus for a markedly different document (maximal contrast) or for a comparatively similar statement-event (minimal contrast). The orientation to maximal contrast makes it possible gradually to record the total spectrum of the discourse(s) within a corpus and thus to work out several discourses on a single theme, or the heterogeneous components within a single discourse. Minimal contrast focuses on reconstructing as accurately and fully as possible each partial area that is being recorded, until the analysis finally appears to be 'saturated'. It is important here to pay constant attention to the comparability or relatedness of the selected documents or part-documents; only in this way are consistent interpretations possible. For example, pamphlets and newspaper reports differ in a variety of ways, as textual genres, in respect of their addressees, in content structure and in the goals they pursue. An analysis of these different data types must take account of this so that no 'slant ' occurs or the different modes of articulation of discourses are not mixed in without due consideration. The selection process of theoretical sampling is carried out until further analyses yield no further knowledge about the total corpus or the research

---

questions that were asked of it. The results of the detailed analyses are then aggregated to provide general statements about the discourse(s).

4.4 Other Data Formats and Methods

Discourse research is characterized – like all qualitative empirical social research – by being strongly text-centred. This is true in several respects: on the one hand the origin of the data themselves is rarely looked at; in most cases they simply become, as complete 'natural documents', the basis for reconstruction – despite the often formulated claim that it is precisely the social production of the particular documents (or utterances) that should be analyzed. On the other hand audio-visual statement-formats (i.e. pictures, sounds, films and so on), as well as artefacts, have hitherto played a marginal role. At this point we can only formulate a few further suggestions on this. The perspectivizing arrangement of different methodological procedures and databases for an overall analysis is normally discussed in qualitative social research under the term 'triangulation' (Flick 2009: 443ff). Ultimately no recipes of success can be recommended for this.

Discourse Analysis and Discourse Research

Discourse research oriented to discourse theory is mostly concerned with written formats and communication processes via the media, whereas 'traditional' ethnomethodologically based Discourse Analysis (DA), that is, talk and conversation research extended to include content elements, has as its research object immediate oral processes of communication, even when – as in critical Discourse Analysis – it has an elaborate foundation in discourse theory. In recent times there have been attempts to build bridges between DA and discourse theory. Such approaches are important to the extent that DA concerns itself with content that is actualized in communicative processes, sees these processes as sedimented or adapted components from discourses, and – like discourse theory – addresses the individual communicative processes that underlie its data material.[8]

---

[8]See in particular Gee (1999), Gee, Hull and Lankshear (1996), Wetherell (1998), Wetherell, Taylow and Jates (2001a), Jørgensen and Philipps (2002), Philipps and Hardy (2002) and Guilhaumou (2010); on conversation research see also Bergmann (2004) and the literature cited in Chapter 2.2.

Discourse Ethnography

A more powerful contribution to the analysis of discursive and non-discursive practices and the material form of *dispositifs* can be achieved through the development of an approach within discourse research – Discourse Ethnography – that goes further than the Ethnography of Communication (Savile-Troike 2003; Cameron 2001: 53ff) currently widely used in qualitative research. Discourse ethnography allows the investigator to make accessible unfolding processes of discourse production and discourse reception. Ethnography is understood here as an approach that is characterized 'by the adoption of an inward-looking perspective, the investigation of a naturalistic field of social practice and the use of observer participation, and these are applied in differing combinations with other methodologies' (Knoblauch 2001: 131, see also Lüders 2004; Hirschauer and Amann 1997; Knoblauch 2005a). For the purposes of discourse research it is a matter of adapting strategies of a 'focused ethnography': this focusing reflects, in Knoblauch's opinion, 'a social development, the units of which are not, in this case, – as in the ethnology paradigm – whole life-communities but contexts of action and communication.' It asks questions about the 'situational or milieu-based or institutional typology' of types of action, forms of problem-solving or interactional patterns (Knoblauch 2001: 137). This kind of ethnography could focus on different relations to discourses in the field of observation. In particular this means, for example, an ethnographically based detailed analysis of the discursive and non-discursive practices in discourse production, in the setting up and using of *dispositifs*, the practical reception/adaptation/confrontation with discourses and the analysis of the interplay between situational contexts and practices with discourses or the constitution of contexts through discourses. The investigation of the practice-locations of discourse production and reproduction can connect with the scientific and techno-sociological laboratory research conducted by Karin Knorr-Cetina, Bruno Latour and others. (See, for example, Latour 1987, Latour and Woolgar 1988, Knorr-Cetina 1981). The concept of 'translation' developed by Michael Callon, Bruno Latour and others within the framework of actor-network-theory may be used to reconstruct the transformation of discourse-specific statements into practices (for example, of dealing with patients, clients, and so on) and technologies/artefacts (such as the construction of rooms, furnishings and the like in old people's homes and similar places). Examples of discourse-analysis investigations of these kinds of 'physical texts' are to be found in Parker and The Bolton Discourse Network (1999: 115ff). Another source that is helpful in the conception of an ethnography of discursive practices is Knoblauch's proposal for the analysis of 'Cultures of Communication' (Knoblauch 1995). Here it is in no sense a matter of a naïve subordination of the complete formation of concrete situations and modes of action by means of discourses or *dispositifs*. It is, rather, a question of possible processes of co-constitution, of actualization, of positioning towards discourses in concrete fields of practice. In this sense ethnography could ultimately come to occupy an important corrective position vis-à-vis discourse research and preserve it from idealistic false conclusions – namely taking a short cut from discourse to practice. Firsthand contact with the field of investigation and the experience of ethnographic fieldwork makes it possible to account for the multiple techniques for situational reception, modification, withdrawal, subversive avoidance and internal distancing in relation to discourses. Such 'dealings with discourse' show up even in 'total institutions' (Goffman 1974), in organizations, in institutional fields and in the 'everyday world'. Of course these only set up their concrete possibilities and specific features in confrontation with the former.[9]

Analysis of Audio-visual Data

The analysis of audio-visual data is very demanding, but is now becoming more and more straightforward because of the 'digital revolution' (Harper 2004; Denzin 2004; Flick 2009: 239–254) – we can observe an explosion in all disciplines in the analysis of visual phenomena (e.g.

---

[9]On this see the study of African-American neighbourhoods by Modan (2007). The interpretative tradition that WDA relates to used ethnographic procedures from the outset and takes account of the fact that actors are not 'marionettes' or 'discursive dopes' (like Garfinkel's 'cultural dopes', which addressed 'actors according to Talcott Parsons'). It is rather the case that social actors relate reflexively to interpretative processes in situations, according to emerging problems and problematizations, or irritations concerning the established criteria of relevance (Alfred Schütz). Poststructuralist perspectives, carrying Marxist or discourse-deterministic elements (i.e Althusser's concept of 'Interpellation'), have problems to account for such as practical divergences and have to give good reasons for ethnographic research. Judith Butler, in her rich and many-facetted work, is struggling vigorously with such questions. A closer look at interpretative traditions in sociology might solve many of her problems.

Raab 2008; Burri 2008; Manghani, Piper and Simon 2006; Smith 2008; Rose 2007; and Sachs-Hombach and Rehkämper as early as 2000). Foucault had already incorporated both linguistic signs and pictures or graphics in his concept of the statement (for example, at the beginning of *Les Mots et les Choses* [*The order of things*] in his analysis of *Las Maninas*; Foucault 1991c). For discourse research particular challenges arise in the form of the comparatively large number of analyzed documents. Expensive individual analyses of pictures, text-picture arrangements and audio-visual formats (such as films), whether they appear in the 'genuine media' or on the Web, may be considered an obstacle to the aims of more comprehensive analysis. For this reason there is a major challenge here in the question of which elements of the analysis should actually be used for the reconstruction of the statement content and in respect of the particular research questions. For this the literature we have already cited and which will be cited below provides many suggestions for the analysis of pictorial motifs, the characteristics of particular genres, the composition and elements of pictures, the multi-modality of picture/text/sound interrelations, but of course these must be used selectively. In much the same way as with the more precisely explained interpretative and analytical fine analysis of textual data (see below), we may also distinguish the investigation of formal (genre) structures and stylistic features, of structure of phenomena, interpretative patterns and narrative patterns. Discussion and sample representations of the procedure in the interpretative-hermeneutic analysis of pictorial data are to be found in social science hermeneutics (e.g. Knoblauch, Schnettler, Raab and Soeffner 2006; Knoblauch et al. 2008; Marotzki and Niesyto 2006; Bohnsack 2008; Raab 2008; Breckner 2010; see also several contributions in Flick, Kardorff and Steinke 2004). In the context of media and communication research, various methodological ideas for the analysis of films and television broadcasts have been put forward, which link interpretative strategies with the analytical reconstruction of the make-up of a film (e.g. Faulstich 1988, Hickethier 2001, Korte and Drexler 2000, Mikos 2008, Mikos and Wegener 2005).

In English-speaking countries Cultural Studies in particular and, more recently, Social Semiotics have pushed forward the analysis of appropriate data formats and, in the tradition of structuralist-semiotic perspectives, have given a stronger emphasis to the analytical dissection of the individual components and structural patterns and also created occasional links to discourse research (Müller-Doohm 1996; Kellner 1995; Hepp 1999; Hepp and Winter 1999; Parker and The Bolton Discourse Network 1999: 65ff; Rose 2001; van Leeuwen and Jewitt 2001; Kress and van Leeuwen 2006; Sturken and Cartwright 2005; van Leeuwen 2005, 2008; Rose 2007; Smith 2008). In the historical sciences, following the works of Aby Warburg and Erwin Panofsky a number of methodological procedures in the interpretation of pictures and art were developed (Bätschmann 2001), which are also being used in current interdisciplinary approaches. Present-day 'Visual Methodologies' (see the comprehensive survey of this in Rose 2007) normally use very diverse analytical strategies; the question of bringing together the particular resulting components for purposes of Discourse Analysis, however, still seems wide open or requires appropriate new justification.[10]

---

[10]But see Link (1982, 1997) who was already analyzing linguistic pictures and graphics. In the context of discourse research, see also the discussions in Maasen, Mayerhauser and Renggli (2006) and Keller and Truschkat (2012). The linguistic sciences are currently also looking definitely at text-picture relationships and 'multi-modal discourses' (Kress and van Leeuwen 2001). A very convincing approach has been developed by Adele Clarke (2005) in her chapter on 'Visual discourses'.

FIVE

The Detailed Analysis of Data

The mode of procedure in data analysis is oriented to the open research logic of qualitative social research (Flick 2009). The methodological proposals below offer assistance in the structuring of the process of interpretation and analysis. They do not constitute any guarantee or prescription for successful research. Following the stylization chosen by Dreyfus and Rabinow (1982) for Michel Foucault, I also refer to *Interpretative Analytics* (Keller 2005b). This includes, referring to a single utterance or discursive event, the analysis of its situational state and material form, the analysis of its formal and linguistic-rhetorical structure, and the interpretative and analytical reconstruction of the contents of the statement.[1] Initially it is a matter of accessing the context of a statement, and then of different strategies for detailed analysis, including the use of qualitative textual software and the possibilities for quantification. The different options and stages in the fine analysis will be outlined below. For the reasons already given, there will be no detailed discussion here of linguistic methods.

Using the questions about the *what* and *how* of the content, the meaning dimensions of a statement (that is: the accessible 'typical core' of individual discursive events and utterances) or discourse will be addressed together with the modes of its occurrence. The use of language – terms (categories), classifications, pictorial representations (graphics), metaphors, arguments, actor-markers, action-markers, and so on – always points to a meaning horizon

---

[1]The ordering and weighting given to the processing of these dimensions may vary; on 'triangulation perspectives' see Flick (2009: 443ff).

or context in which it makes sense and which is produced through this use itself. Every use of language, therefore, suggests a *specific* existence of worldly phenomena. The accessing of such content must compress, more or less strongly, or standardize the original utterances, for example into the form of narrative structures or plots, meaning patterns, topoi and interpretative repertoires. Meanings do not, therefore, exist in discourses as loose unrelated semiotic particles, but in structured forms, as pre-typified components of collective knowledge that may, from the perspective of the observation, be re-typified in the process of reconstruction. For the analysis of the meaning components of a discourse there are a number of theoretically well-founded and, in terms of both methodology and ideas, well-developed proposals, for instance as meaning patterns, interpretative schemes, storyline and interpretative repertoire in Keller (1998);[2] as 'frames', 'framing and reasoning devices' and 'storylines' in Gamson and Modigliani (1987), Donati (2011), or Ferree, Gamson, Gerhards and Rucht (2002); as narrative structures in Viehöver (2010, 2011); as 'tropes' and 'topic' in Knoblauch (2011) or Wengeler (2003); and in the context of the cognitive sciences we also find 'cultural models', i.e. cognitive 'schemata' or 'scripts' (Gee 1999).

The analysis of individual data begins with simple or repeated reading, and paraphrasing of the content may also be connected to this.

Achim Landwehr (2001: 113ff), in his Introduction to Historical Discourse Analysis, brings together different proposals for methodological procedure that had been put forward in linguistic Discourse Analysis, for instance, by Teun van Dijk and others: van Dijk (1997a, b) makes a distinction between the analysis of the macrostructure and the microstructure of a text. The investigation of the macrostructure of a text is related to its external, formal, overall configuration, and its elements are the theme, the formal structure and the representative principles. The analysis of a number of texts makes it possible to outline the corresponding macrostructure of the discourse: 'What

---

[2]In German, the term 'Deutungsmuster' refers to typified meaning patterns or interpretative schemes which organize the way we interpret situations and act according to such interpretations. I use it much as the Anglo-Saxon notion of 'frame'. But unlike the use of the frame concept, e.g. in social movement research (see Chapter 2.5), 'Deutungsmuster' does not assume a 'cognitive component and localisation' or a necessarily strategic use; it refers to social patterns of meaning, circulating in societies.

linguistic features are at the centre, what words, arguments, boundaries are found repeatedly, hold the discourse together and constitute the core of conflicts and disagreements?' (Landwehr 2001: 116). The investigation of the microstructure of a single text, conversely, aims at its 'internal' structure, at features of the argumentation, style and rhetoric, that is to say, elements that point to texts as actions that intend to make an effect. Arguments, on the one hand, may have a factual logical character, and on the other hand an emotionalizing and appellative one. One important component of rhetorical or argument analysis is the reconstruction of the rules of derivation (topoi); furthermore, the analysis of rhetoric also includes the investigation of the function of various tropes, (metaphors, irony, metonymy, synecdoche) and so on.

For individual analysis, proposals from the grounded theory research programme are again helpful. These include, apart from the theoretical sampling mentioned above, the ideas of coding, commentaries and memos. Here it is not a question of adopting these concepts in discourse research in a 1:1 relationship; it is rather that as sensitizing options they require a more or less comprehensive adaptation for the purposes of Discourse Analysis.[3] The various strategies of (qualitative) coding aim at a conceptual 'compression' of individual textual passages within documents in both an analytical-structuring and also an interpretative respect (see 5.3 below). The direction or the goal of this compression is predetermined in discourse research by the specific research questions and related concepts (e.g. components of structure of phenomena, subject positions, practices, meaning patterns). In commentaries (small accompanying notes) it can and should be noted why a particular code was formulated and related to a textual passage. The term *memos* refers to more or less comprehensive notes made during the research process, in which it is noted what further considerations, ideas, flashes of insight and hypotheses arise in respect of a specific textual passage or coding. Memos are therefore components of a notebook that accompany a research programme. A detailed analysis mostly takes place in several stages, which oscillate to and from the text: starting with the reading of individual documents, one advances to paraphrasing, to contextual analysis and analytical

[3]Initially this only means that not all of the stages in Grounded Theory have to be taken over, but that the concepts present there can be treated as tools that are adapted to the questions and methodological steps in discourse research (see Clarke 2005).

dissection, to precise detailed interpretation and finally to summarizing. For the processing of individual texts there is a broad spectrum of highly varied text analysis procedures available.[4] A selected number of these will be illustrated in more detail below.

5.1 The Situational and Material Nature of a Statement

Analyses of discourse prefer to deal with natural data and combine the analysis of such materials with the investigator's own data collection and the fieldwork soundings outlined above. Social science discourse research, however, is not purely textual research: it is concerned with the social relationship between linguistic or semiotic usage and meaning production as the basis for the objectivization of social knowledge. An important first investigative step, therefore, in respect of individual statement-events, is the analysis of their positional state in a range of situational, institutional-organizational and social contexts (see text box).

On Distinguishing Contextual Dimensions

- *historical-social, temporal-diagnostic context*: in what historical and social context – specified in terms of the research question – were the statements made or the data (texts) produced? What are the most important features?
- *institutional-organizational context*: in what institutional field and organizational setting did the data arise? What are the particular structural features, rules and textual formats of this field? In what kind of edition and for what readership were the texts conceived? How are they disseminated? What linguistic forms, themes, and power-relationships are characteristic of this field?
- *situative context*: who is named as the concrete author, publisher or responsible person for a document? From what institutional, organizational and situative position was the text conceived? What is the concrete relationship between productive and receptive context, and the situations of speaking, writing and recording?

---

[4]See Hitzler and Honer (1997), Titscher, Wodak, Meyer and Vetter (2000).

In this we may start from the questions of *who* produces a statement *how, where* and *for whom*? What is recorded are the positions and relations of statement-producers and recipients; institutional settings and their rules; staged and 'natural' events which become stimuli for the production of statements (e.g. catastrophes, processes of parliamentary decision-making, university reforms and other 'emergencies'); the media contexts where they appear (e.g. text-books, popular science books, newspapers, discussions, television reports, the Internet); more general social contexts (economic, scientific, socio-cultural activities); and finally also existing power-constellations in a discursive field. The different contextual levels have a funnel-shaped relationship with one or more documents within a corpus. In this investigative step it is important not to suppose too hastily, on the basis of prior knowledge or prejudice, that there is a direct relationship between context and the textual document, but to study the two dimensions independently from an analytical point of view, or determine their relationship only during the process of the analysis.

The question of the material form of a statement is to do with the mode of its occurrence: in other words, to its manner of articulation and dissemi-nation. This may include, for example, text-type, edition, publisher, mode of distribution or reception arena – are we concerned with a parliamentary speech, with a newspaper text, with a book, or with a television documen-tary? How large is the scope of the particular document? Who may poten-tially be reached through it? What resources have gone into the production of the utterance? In what institutional power-field does it appear?

5.2 Formal and Linguistic-Rhetorical Structure

I use the term *formal structure* of an utterance to refer to its features as a document of a particular communicative or textual genre. Textbooks, docu-mentary films, newspaper commentaries, news reports and so on are, for us, recognizable and distinct by virtue of their relatively conventionalized structure. In particular, media and communication research has identified corresponding features of the genres.[5] The particular conventional formal rules for these genre-types function as structural frameworks for what can be included under the heading of content. They also shape the 'allowed'

---

[5]On news items, see van Dijk (1988); on communicative genres, see Knoblauch and Luckmann (2004).

ways of (re)presenting such content. Corresponding questions relate to the theme and the composition of its treatment (form and structure). Closely linked to this are the possibilities for the linguistic-rhetorical, dramatic and audio-visual treatment of a statement, that is to say, questions of rhetoric, the 'style' of utterance and presentation – the analytical reconstruction of which is always simultaneously an interpretative process. And the result of this may turn out differently, depending on the attitude of the reader. It should therefore be treated with appropriate caution: is it a matter of a factual argument, of polemic, emotionalized or appellative presentations? Are pictures, metaphors and so on, involved? What different graphic and formal elements are applied and how is this done? How are they interrelated? What rules of reasoning and argumentation are presented? What is the link between elements that are cognitive (fact-related) or moralizing, or based on moral and aesthetic value judgements? What role is played by the use of tropes (synonyms, metaphors, synecdoche, irony and so on)?[6]

5.3 The Interpretative Analytics of Contents

The interpretative and analytical recording and reconstruction of statements is closely related to the step we have just described and frequently marks the difference between linguistic and social science analyses of discourse. It focuses on the production of a detailed matrix or a schematized record of the statement that serves as the basis for interpretative hypothesis-formation concerning the content, functioning and effects of a discourse. Following the process of distinguishing between the subjective, situational and socially typical meaning of an utterance, as it is done within the framework of hermeneutic sociology of knowledge, the major concern in this process of reconstruction is the level of social typology. The level of subjective meaning attribution is of secondary importance for the programme of discourse research followed here. Discourse research does not enquire about any authentic subjective intention and (idiosyncratic) meaning of an utterance for producers of texts. It considers the situational meaning content

---

[6]See Gamson's approach stylistic-rhetorical structure is dealt with under the heading of 'framing devices' (see Chapter 2.5 above). On the meaning of tropes in academic writing on history see White (1975); on the role of metaphors, in particular, see Link (1984); on collective symbolism see Link (2011).

in the direct context of an utterance, but focuses ultimately on the general content, in the way it may be described within the framework of a social collective. The link between the situational and general levels also makes it possible to recognize and reflect different ways of using typifications. For example, the interpretation of an event as a 'catastrophe' can be linked to a variety of inferences – better technology, abandonment of a particular path of technical development, inevitable fate. During the reconstruction process a number of main questions may be asked about the context of the individual utterance: what is the theme of the text? In what categories, arguments, classifications[7] and so on is it being dealt with? What sub-themes are introduced as relevant? What are the core components of the utterance? Are there any typical examples, repetitions of utterances or terminology? What meaning is attributed to the vocabulary employed as compared to other terms used in the particular field of discourse? What kind of statement (in Foucaults' sense) is to be found on the surface of the utterance?

For the interpretative-analytical dissection of texts several approaches are available. This is also true of the presentation of single and overall results, perhaps in tabular form, as continuous text, graphics or in the form of a 'tree-diagram', or a semantic network. Three proposals and possible, mutually complementary reconstruction perspectives for individual documents are described below. Firstly, this is to do with the analytical description of the *phenomenon or problem structure* that is articulated in the text, next with the *meaning patterns (interpretative schemes, frames;* 'Deutungsmustert') that link individual utterance elements, and finally with the *narrative patterns* that organize the content of an utterance.[8] Following this I shall discuss briefly the concept of *cultural models*. The results of the different stages in the detailed data analysis must be related to one another in an interpretative process of triangulation. Ultimately it will depend on the research questions, which of

---

[7]Classifications are an institutionally stabilized form of processes of social typification, and for discourse research they are of great significance because of their 'world-ordering' function. What is important, in addition to the structural fact of classification is their 'performative' effect, such as when administrative ethnic categorizations become the basis for self-description and the identity politics of ethnic grouping, or only create such groups because of the classification itself, as has been described, for instance, in gender research and various investigations of 'identity politics' or 'racial formations' (Bowker and Leigh Star 2000; Link 1997; Keller 2005a; Omi and Winant 1994).

[8]On this see the whole of Keller (2005a); on the location of interpretative analytics in social science hermeneutics, see Keller (2005b).

---

the three analytical possibilities that we have sketched – or others that we have not mentioned – will be employed, and how they will be combined. With regard to the interpretative-analytical fine analysis, the *grounded theory* perspective mentioned above again has helpful suggestions to make concerning the practical handling of the data material.[9]

A variety of software-programs for qualitative data analysis (e.g. ATLAS/ti, MaxQDA, PROSPERO) may be used to assist in data management and analysis. For this the data to be processed must be available in a digitized form (for example, from Internet databases, or as scanned documents). The available programs rely mostly on the conceptual and procedural bases of grounded theory. They make it possible to construct and administer codes, memos and so on, and, unlike card index methods, they facilitate survey compilations of codings, accompanying commentaries and textual references or citations. Word frequency counts and certain other quantitative assessments can also be conducted using programs of this sort. The relationship of effort (e.g. in scanning) to yield certainly depends on the particular data material and its condition; and possible new constraints and restrictions that arise from the use of a program must also be reflected in the research process. The rapid and sorted overview, for instance, of the different utterance components that are attributed to one or more codes, may facilitate, advance and stimulate the interpretation of data and formation of hypotheses – but it cannot replace the analytical work of the investigator. Even in this type of software-based data application, the direct confrontation between the analyst and the data remains the central ground of research. A helpful introduction into the use of qualitative acquisition software is provided by Diaz-Bone and Schneider (2010); for a more comprehensive survey see Corbin and Strauss (2008).

5.3.1 Phenomenal Structure

The concept of *phenomenal structure* relates to the fact that discourses, in the constitution of their referential relationship (or their 'theme') designate a variety of elements and combine them into a specific form of constitution of phenomena, a structure or constellation of a problem. For example, in a public debate on a problem, the different dimensions of an action-problem

---

[9]On this see Strauss and Corbin (1998); a brief account is also to be found in Titscher, Wodak, Meyer and Vetter (2000: 74ff); with regard to Discourse Analysis see also Keller (2010, 2011b), Clarke (2005).

must always be dealt with by the protagonists; this includes determining the nature of the problem or theme of an utterance unit, designating the causal relationships (cause–effect), responsibilities, problem-dimensions, value-implications, moral and aesthetic values, consequences, action possibilities and so on (Gerhards 1992; Schetsche 1996). The actual components of this kind of problem structure are not known before the factual analysis, but must be ascertained from the empirical data, and there they must transcend the singular utterance. In this respect individual data usually contain only partial elements.

Example:	Phenomenal or Problem Structure in hegemonic discourse in French debates on waste as the aggregated result of a number of fine analyses (Keller 1998: 232)

Problem-structure: Administrative discourse on waste: sociotechnical modernization

Causes	Waste as a 'cleanliness problem'; Discrepancy between quantities available and disposal or utilization infrastructure:
	– growth in wealth, economic and technical progress, consumption requirements of the users → increase in waste occurrence
	– waste as a problem of deficient rubbish disposal in dumps
	– waste as a problem of a lack of civic responsibility and discipline
	– waste as a problem of national balance of payments/ use of raw materials
	– waste as a problem of conditions of international competition
Responsibility	Politics/ State Administration (has to develop and implement outline programmes of waste policy in agreement with commerce)
	– regional authorities, firms (have to implement political decisions in an autonomous way)
	– citizens/society (have to abandon irrational fears, egoistic refusal; have to take up responsibility for waste and accept proposed expert technologies for solution)

(Continued)

(Continued)

Need for Action and mode of Problem-solving	Low problem-level; technical mastery of waste situation is possible by means of requirement/recycling/utilization and removal. Measures: – large-scale technical expansion and optimization of the disposal and recycling/utilization infrastructure – creating acceptance of the disposal infrastructure through communication and participation – comprehensive mobilization of civic responsibility (communities, business, consumers)
Self-positioning	Representatives of scientific/technical, economic and pragmatic reasoning, of civilizing (socio-cultural/technical) progress; the state as observer of collective interest
Positioning of opposite Others	– civic actors (local authorities, commerce, citizens) display a lack of awareness of responsibility, irrational fears and repression – irrationality and fundamentalism in (German) waste-management policies, cloak to hide economic protectionism
Object culture	Not a subject for discussion of waste; pursues unavailable modernization dynamics and market rationalities
Welfare model	material welfare model; freedom of needs (production and consumption)
Reference Values	– State guarantees collective interest (welfare, progress, modernity) – (factual and moral) cleanliness of public space – nature as a (scarce national) resource, the use of which can be optimized – identity of contemporary form of society and the 'good life'

The analytical description of phenomenal structures – which, in the course of discourses, will certainly change in time – is directed at two things:

1 The dimensional access to the phenomenon: The general dimensions from which the phenomenon is discursively constituted may resemble or differ from each other, more or less strongly, in a field of discourse between various mutually competing discourses. They are captured in an abstracting form, for

example in such a way that it can be ascertained whether causal relationships, self labelling or labelling by others (identity markers), attribution of responsibility, solution requirements and so on are introduced as relevant dimensions by the discourse itself. In terms of grounded theory the concern is with the development of 'codes', i.e. the generation of abstract categories for the designation of individual utterance, and thus discourse constituents, through the different stages of open, axial and selective coding (see Strauss and Corbin 1998, Strauss 1987: 55ff), with detailed explanations, guideline questions, sample analyses and so on).[10] The different ways in which this is carried out, that is to say, whether, for example, primary and secondary causes or consequences are distinguished, depend upon the research questions.

2 *The content implementation of the dimensions*: completion of the content of the reconstructed dimensions may vary according to the occasion or type of discourse. It is described in a condensed form: not by means of a simple summary recording of 'original quotations' – which could definitely be used for purposes of representation or illustration – but, if possible, with regard to its general (or generalizable) elements. Through the analysis of the different utterances it is possible to reconstruct *coding families,* i.e. attributions of various characteristic features to the corresponding code-category, such as causes, consequences, correlations, boundary conditions, processes, types, identities and so on (Glaser 1978).[11] Phenomenal structures may be represented in tabular form (e.g. Gamson and Lasch 1983; Donati 2011; Hajer 1995: 164ff; Keller 1998: 209ff; Viehöver 2011; Diaz-Bone 2008: 421ff) or using the visualization models of cognitive anthropology.

---

[10]So that this does not cause any irritation: the adaptation of some of the procedural proposals of grounded theory for the purposes of discourse research requires a number of terminological and conceptual 'translations'; this is as a result of the differing research interests: the authors of grounded theory are primarily interested in the investigation of social action or practice contexts (such as interaction processes and human-machine interactions in hospitals. Their questions and examples are formulated accordingly. For discourse research it is a matter of analyzing social production and the structuring of discourses on the basis of (primarily) textual data. The ideas of grounded theory must be applied accordingly. Strauss himself – like Peirce, Mead or Alfred Schütz, too (see Chapter 2.1) – speaks occasionally of the 'universe of discourse' and corresponding areas of symbolic confrontation (Strauss 1991). See also the whole of Keller (2005a, 2011b, 2013) and Clarke (2005).

[11]On the procedures involved in coding see Strauss and Corbin (1998); Strauss (1987); Flick (2009: 305ff); Titscher, Wodak, Meyer and Vetter (2000: 76ff); on applications in Discourse Analysis cf. Diaz-Bone (2008: 198ff), Viehöver (2010).

Procedures in Coding according to grounded theory (related, in discourse research, to phenomenal structure, meaning patterns and narrative structures)

'Rules of Thumb'

Do not simply paraphrase the sentences of a document, but discover genuine categories and label these, at least provisionally

Put these categories, as specifically and variably as possible, into a relationship with their conditions, consequences, strategies (...)

Put these categories into a relationship with sub-categories (...)

Do this on the basis of specific data, and refer to these frequently, by recording page number, quotations or summaries directly in the coding notes

Underline key areas of concern, this facilitates reviewing and later sorting

If the key category (or categories) begins to become clear, or is already clear, then you should make sure that all categories and sub-categories can be related to one another and to the key category/categories

Later the subordinate categories which show little or no relation to other categories, with their associated hypotheses may be discarded as more or less irrelevant in respect of the integrated result of the analysis (...); or else the researcher must try to relate these categories specifically to his analysis. (Strauss 1998: 122f; see Strauss 1987: 81ff)

Basic Coding Questions:

(from the summary of Titscher, Wodak, Meyer and Vetter 2000: 79ff)

Open Coding:

What actually happens in the text?
What category does the textual passage suggest?

Axial Coding:

What are the conditions for the events comprised in the concept?
How can the interaction between the actors be described?
What strategies and tactics can be determined?
What are the consequences of the events?

DOING DISCOURSE RESEARCH

Selective Coding:

What is the most striking feature of the field of investigation?
What do I consider to be the main problem?
What is the central theme of the story?
Which phenomena are represented again and again in the data?

The interpretative-analytical recording of the elements adhering to a phe-nomenal structure and appearing in a singular utterance happens throughout different coding steps; it is a matter of a structured process of textual analysis. The particular reasons for the allocation of coding terms may be recorded in the form of memos, that is to say, more or less systematized accompany-ing notes.[12] In this procedure, analysing word-by-word, sentence-by-sentence and/or sequence-by-sequence, the researcher works out the references to and dimensions of 'the reality of the world', which a discourse opens up, proposes and performs, all this in more or less explicit ways. Admittedly at this point in an analysis these references are comparatively unconnected. It is only through the reconstruction of the common theme, the storyline or the 'plot', which links them and meshes them into a specifically meaningful relationship, that this stage in the analysis is completed (see below). The following overview illustrates, using extracts, the interrelation between codes, commentaries and memos. Dealing with the relevant textual documents and so on is made easier through the use of qualitative text-processing software.[13]

An Example: Coding, Memo and Source-text in Rainer Diaz-Bone (2008)

For example, in his research on music styles Diaz-Bone (2008) used concepts of coding and memo as follows:

Scope: a corpus from the music periodical *METAL HAMMER*, consisting of 33 large primary documents (each consisting of a compilation of many articles), in which 151 codes were allocated, 2018 textual locations marked, and 35 memos composed

(Continued)

---

[12]This procedure is supported by a number of qualitative software packages.

[13]I am indebted to Rainer Diaz-Bone for allowing the use of his working documents.

Explanation of the Code 'Working Ethos'

'The complex of production (code) includes the aspect of the represented working ethos (subcode), i.e. the thematization of the attitude that musicians display or the motives of production that are represented in the discourse. This code was introduced when it became evident that this was a theme in the *METAL HAMMER* periodical. The code was developed step by step. Initially it was commented on in such a way that the analytical handling could be checked; I have therefore noted what always had to be observed, and what could be marked. After this I determined in a complete overview what occurs and what is striking. The code was allocated to 91 places in the text; it was interrelated with four additional codes (e.g. value/concept: perfection, precisions, technique; value/concept: professionalism, and others)'

Immediate Code-Commentary (Extract)

'The work ethos is, indeed, a main code but it carries the risk of over-hasty reliance on the mentalities or ethical state of groups, without taking the essential interim step of ensuring that (1) it is a question here of a 'represented ethic' and (2) that this represented ethic is developed in a network of cultural knowledge concepts which give it content. Therefore, the interpretative strategy is: first the analysis of concepts and then those of its networking and of the ethic that is established represented in it. What is striking here is : professionalism, i.e. the activity of musicians would also be regarded as entertainment (4x); to make the kind of music that can be played and mastered (!) (2x); practice: practise a lot to uncover weaknesses (in instrument articles), technical weaknesses are not forgiven! (again in instrument articles); to put on a respectable (!) show, the audience will sweat accordingly. The audience must be worked hard every day. (...)'

Example: Original textual passage that was assigned for the code 'Working Ethos':

'In this connection there can be no more talk of "playing around" than in current production. The Bremen "Wolves" have rather the reputation of belonging to the extremely demanding species. "What we have brought about in the way of self-criticism and hardness on ourselves is bordering on masochism", howls the head wolf. "At the end of a week we were already able to produce the best guitar sounds we have ever had, but that didn't keep us from experimenting further. Sometimes a dozen different guitars were piling up in the studio and as many amplifiers in the 'financial suicide' price bracket (...) And we checked all these gadgets again in all possible and impossible variations, and recorded over takes that had already been checked out."'

Extract from the memo on the code-complex 'Instruments' (the complete memo takes several pages)

'The production of instruments: is the handicraft aspect of their production emphasized here? What about the materials? The XX-advertising (MH-02-99–131) stresses the link between technology and craftsmanship. What are the normal ways of playing? There is a description of how guitars are tuned lower so that the harmonies change. "The accusation I hear most often is that our harmonies are not correct, and our guitars are out of tune. But it has to be like this, not because that is our idea, but because these songs grow organically and in the end sound just like life which also doesn't consist only of harmony and agreement." (MH-03-99-BAND-030). In the sound description it is noticeable: the instruments are described like actors or performers who have entrances, who interact, who are in a relationship to one another. The formally describable musical elements, in contrast, are hardly described at all (MH-03-99-STUD-020).'

5.3.2 Meaning Patterns (Interpretation Schemata and Frames)[14]

The constitution and processing of the theme or reference phenomenon of a discourse can then, after successful analysis of the phenomenal structure, also be reconstructed with regard to the discourse-specific actualization and the link with general meaning patterns that are available in the context of a knowledge-community or in a given 'universe of discourse'. Here it is a matter of the interpretation schemata or frames which are accessible for individual and collective interpretative work in social knowledge and which are updated in event-related interpretative processes. Discourses build on a number of meaning patterns that are available in social stocks of knowledge, or they may constitute and spread new ones, anchor them in such stocks of knowledge. They process particular (specific) combinations of such patterns which show up all together or (more often only) partially, or manifest themselves in linguistic (or visual etc.) utterances. The concept of 'meaning pattern' (interpretative scheme, frame) aims at the statement level of an utterance, at those kinds of core elements that can be labelled as 'socially

---

[14]All terms here refer to the German 'Deutungsmuster'.

typified' in a given social context – i.e., temporarily conventionalized or fixed meaning figures in social collectives. Unlike the previously described analytical-coding dissection of an utterance, this is a question of investigating the configuration of the relationship between specific components of the utterance in terms of its nature as 'statement': a meaning pattern links various sense making elements into a coherent (not necessarily consistent) meaning-figure that may appear in various manifestations.[15]

The different analytical steps in meaning-pattern reconstruction may similarly be oriented to the proposals of grounded theory[16] as well as sequential and analytical interpretative strategies from the context of social science hermeneutics. The reconstruction of phenomenal or problem structure by means of coding processes, as described above, may serve as a first preparatory step. In this way it is possible to capture those dimensions of an utterance which may be considered as relevant, depending on the particular research questions. These might be, for example, the categories of problem causation, threatening consequences, solution-options, the differently involved actors, positioning of self and others, appearing value commitments and to all those elements' corresponding sub-categories, and so on, all of which do not necessarily have to occur in a single utterance. For example, as in the public debate on the problem of household waste (Keller 1998), technology may be understood as a contribution to solving the problem or as merely shifting the problem, and treated accordingly in a number of newspaper articles.

For the reconstruction of meaning patterns those passages are selected, within the text under investigation, which, as a result of the coding process, contain data on the dimension in question. For instance, if a textual component has been given the code 'problem-solution: technology' then this section (and subsequently also others which have been given the same code) is selected for sequential analysis. This may be a matter of several adjacent

---

[15]A good example of this is provided by the analysis of the meaning pattern 'motherly love' that was presented by Yvonne Schütze (1992). Meaning-pattern reconstructions have hitherto been carried out primarily in the context of biographical research or in narrative interviews. See, for example, Reichertz (1997: 44ff), Lüders and Meuser (1997), Meuser and Sackmann (1992), Plaß and Schetsche (2001); as an application in discourse research, Keller (1998, 2010), Truschkat (2008) and Schmied-Knittel (2008). The proceeding of 'frame analysis' suggested by Gamson (see above Chapter 2.5) may be partially adapted as a form of meaning-pattern analysis.

[16]See the keywords 'guidelines', 'detailed analysis' conducted sentence by sentence and 'open coding' in Strauss and Corbin (1998) and Strauss (1987). On the Sequential Analysis discussed below see Flick (2009: 333ff).

---

sentences, of sections, chapters or complete texts. The selected passage, beginning with the first sentence, is then subjected, sentence-by-sentence, to sequential detailed analysis. The principle of sequential analysis consists of developing, with regard to the particular research questions, and following the flow of the text, as many interpretative hypotheses as possible for individual sentences, whole textual sections, or the entire text. These are then checked, rejected or kept and/or refined with regard to their appropriateness in the immediate continuation of the text. Ideally it is a question of a group process, in the course of which particular interpretations are gradually eliminated and a single one is capable of being *socially objectivized* (that is: in a group discussion process; see Strauss 1987: 40ff) as 'fitting'. In this context 'fitting' means that the hypothesis produced or the reconstructed and named meaning pattern, as compared to the rejected meaning patterns, is best suited to characterizing the sense-making content of the passage in question and structures the analyzed coding unit in a particular, discourse-specific way. At the same time the initially rather extensive explanatory work aims at avoiding the danger of the simple projection of the researcher's own prejudices onto the text; it is therefore a question of a strategy of methodological self-control.

Example of the Attribution of Meaning Pattern (frame) and Utterance (Keller 1998)

Technology-Meaning Pattern 'Risk' (German Debate on Waste)

'Branded as the most modern waste incineration works in Germany, if not in the world, a plant in Augsburg costing more than 900 million marks underwent a "warm start-up" in the autumn of last year. Last week the trial run came to an abrupt end. For this words were used that newspaper readers know only with reference to nuclear reactors: cracks in a steam pressure-pipe, leaks in water pipes, quick shutdown. And of course: the legally permitted pollution output into the environment was not exceeded. One should not forget: all technology is subject to breakdowns – and the more complex it is, the more subject to breakdowns – a truism.'

(Süddeutsche Zeitung, 5.5.94)

(Continued)

(Continued)

Explanation: This meaning pattern, which has developed particularly with reference to nuclear energy, works on the basis of the 'normality of catastrophes' (Charles Perrow 1999), the arrival of 'residual risk', the incalculability of incidental consequences (health and environmental risks) and the absence of possibilities for damage avoidance. Technological progress cannot solve these problems, but rather leads to a relocation of hazards. The risk culture that seemed immutable in industrial societies is now being questioned. Technological action strategies are being rejected in favour of political measures.

The labelling of the meaning pattern is carried out by the researcher; in this, terms from the very texts under investigation may sometimes be used. A corresponding analysis of a variety of texts serves the purpose of reconstructing, for a specific research interest, the variations contained in the material and thus determining the patterns that occur in the particular field – perhaps under the guise of different 'types'.[17] This mode of procedure is economical in terms of research effort, to the extent that data-related saturation effects occur comparatively rapidly – the number of variations is limited. It may therefore be enough to analyze a few interviews or texts related to a particular research question to produce an adequate picture of the field of investigation.

5.3.3 Narrative Structure

Different approaches in discourse research emphasize the role of storylines, common themes, plots or narrative patterns by means of which the individual components of an utterance are bound to a smaller or larger narrative or story, that is to say, how they are configured over and above the random sequencing of linguistic utterances.[18] It is only in this way that an utterance gains its inner coherence; and only in this way that complexes of

---

[17]On this see the handling and presentation of the American discourses on affirmative action in Gamson and Lasch (1983).

[18]See, for example, Gamson and Modigliani (1989), Keller (1998). The meaning of narrative patterns for the organization of utterances in scientific texts has meanwhile been examined by various investigators. The development of narrative-oriented approaches within a structuralist perspective was done by Alexandre Greimas using semiotics; within a hermeneutic perspective Paul Ricœur is the central reference; see Ricœur (1990).

statements about dynamic relations, processes and changes are possible. In the reconstruction of narrative patterns it is possible to distinguish different levels of generalization or specification, such as main, subsidiary and sub-narratives. Here too, the analysis of these storylines – as with the previously considered investigative steps – focuses on typical and typifiable patterns, respectively, which are ultimately manifest in a plethora of concrete and distinct utterances and statement forms. In Keller (1998) the term storyline is used to characterize the narrative pattern to which the various meaning components of a discourse are linked. In the empirical procedure narrative elements are mostly subsumed in the process of coding we explained above (see Hajer 1995). An elaborated discourse-oriented approach within narration analysis was introduced by Willy Viehöver (2010, 2011); see text box.

Viehöver (2010: 46ff) proposes assumptions and procedures of narrative analysis of discourses as follows.

Structural Assumptions about Narratives

1 Stories consist of episodes, which may be based on value-oppositions 'which are either expressed through pairs of antonyms such as black/white and so on, or through relations between antagonists (hero : anti-hero).'
2 Narratives 'have personnel at their disposal (actants: hero : anti-hero; sender : receiver; object; assistant).'
3 The individual units and actants used in the narrative 'are linked to one another by a single more or less dramatic action-configuration (the *plot*) (…). Through this configurative act both the meanings of the lexical surface structures and the value structures are organized. What was particularly popular in the discussion of climate was the attempt to tell of the sufferings of the planet by analogy with human sickness: "the Earth is in a fever!" This kind of plot offers a series of possible ways of unfolding the story of global climate change.'

Mode of Procedure in Narrative Analysis

1 'Identification of the individual episodes in the narrative'
2 'Fine analysis of the episodes, the structures of the actors, time and space of the elements in the narrative and their linking through the plot'

(Continued)

(Continued)

3 'Determination of the main objects and value-structures'
4 'Determination of the narratives that are typical of the discourse.'

Example of the Processing of an Individual Text Sequence

'The Malaysian Prime Minister Matathir [*anti-hero*] spoke of "neo-colonialism" [*value-opposition*], which could soon turn into "eco-colonialism" [*value-opposition*]. Germany's Environmental Minister Töpfer [*failing helper*] (nickname: "Eco-Genscher") [*failing hero*] attempted to mediate [*action; active, pragmatic*] between the representatives of North and South [*value-opposition; spatial structure*] – in vain. "If Rio fails" [*value-opposition*], warned [*action; pragmatic*] the Canadian Maurice Strong [*sender*] "this would be the starting signal for a war" [*value-opposition; time-structure: future*] "between rich and poor" [*value-opposition*].'

(*Der Spiegel* [*Helper of the Sender*]
no. 21, 1992: 224. (Author's translation)

In the example above (1) (...) the Malaysian Prime Minister figures as the 'anti-hero' in the climate negotiations, because he describes the supporters of measures against the greenhouse effect as exponents of a kind of neo-colonialism, whereas Maurice Strong (sender and mediator of main values), as a central figure in the Rio Negotiations, warns of the consequences of a failure in the Environmental Conference and thus imparts to its negation (war) a central value in the narrative (peace). Töpfer, in contrast, is represented as a failing helper and mediator between North and South and is commented on ironically (Eco-Genscher).

Another possible way of dealing both with the phenomenal structure and also the narrative patterns inherent to a discourse's network of statements may be found in the context of cognitive anthropology, which works with the concepts of the cultural model and thereby targets cognitive-collective 'schemata', 'scenarios' or 'scripts'. As in Alfred Schütz's concept of 'typification', this is used to characterize an interface between the social construction of knowledge and the cognitive achievements of an individual. In the meantime, as a superordinate term for the different approaches within this field, the concept of the 'cultural model' has established itself.[19] This is used to refer to process-scenarios – such as current storylines or 'film scripts' for situations/actions ('visit to a restaurant', 'going to the authorities', 'courtship') – or to phenomenon-related associations of terms (what is 'coffee', 'tea', a 'beer drinker' and so on), which are considered to be relatively standardized or typified for specific socio-cultural contexts, where this is familiar and 'usable here and now' in the opinion of all participants. They depend in part on life-world related experiential knowledge and practices that are handed down (e.g. as traditions, 'established ways of doing') by others, but they are also produced and processed in discourses (e.g. in pedagogic discourse prescriptions for dealing with unwilling children). They are normally presented in the form of branching and linking 'tree diagrams'.[20]

[19]A discussion of 'cultural models' in the context of discourse research is to be found in Gee (1999). See also D'Andrade (1995), Strauss and Quinn (1997).

[20]It is a matter for discussion whether 'cultural models' are no more than a different form of representation for the organization of phenomenal structure or whether they are a fundamentally different concept. In my opinion the former is true. The general meaning of such scripts and so on were made prominent by Harold Garfinkel (1967), following Alfred Schütz and others, in his experiments with crises. The interface, popularized in anthropology, between cognition and collective interpretative schemata, together with other terms, has long been a basic idea of Schütz and the associated sociology of knowledge (see Strauss and Quinn 1997 on the former; Luckmann 1999 on the latter).

SIX

From Detailed Analysis
to Overall Results

6.1 From Utterances via Statements
to Discourse and Beyond

In discourse research single data units have the status of discourse documents or 'discourse fragments' (Jäger 2009: 188ff). In a document of this type it is not necessarily the case that only a single discourse is represented, nor that it is fully represented. Discourse fragments contain *compatible* partial elements of discourses. To be able to make statements about the discourse(s) in a particular discursive field, the results of individual detailed analyses in the research process need to be aggregated. This is a question of a construction activity on the part of the researchers, which may be understood – by analogy to type-formation in the social sciences – as an abstracting generalization of the particular characteristics of the individual case (Kluge 1999; Kelle and Kluge 1999). From the methodological approach of qualitative social research we cannot know, on an empirical basis, how many different discourses are to be found in a specific field of investigation and by what meaning-elements or rules of formation they are structured. This also applies in the case of prior knowledge of different 'media storehouses' or constellations of actors.[1]

---

[1]For example, in Keller's (1998) investigation of debates on domestic waste in Germany and France it only gradually became visible from the analysis of material that in the French public debate on waste there existed only a single discourse, and a further one only outside the mass media, whereas in the German discussion there were two competing discourses in the public media.

What is significant, therefore, for the reconstruction of whole discourses is the step-by-step procedure and gradual advance by means of a greater or smaller number of individual detailed analyses. As we have already mentioned, it is helpful to orientate oneself with the gradual selection of data for detailed analysis according to the concept of *theoretical sampling* (Strauss and Corbin 1998; Strauss 1987: 38ff). That is to say, one should not work through the documents one by one at random, without due thought, but should select the data in a theory-driven and well-founded way. The criteria of 'minimal' or 'maximal contrast' are important in this respect. The principle of 'minimal contrast' aims to capture a specific discourse (or type) in its full range or a partial phenomenon as follows: Utterances, texts, discursive events, situations and so on that are as similar as possible, or only marginally different, are analysed in succession in order to establish their common pattern. The principle of maximal contrast serves to discover the breadth of the available data by investigating as systematically as possible cases that differ very markedly from one another. This means that after the analysis of a document or a situation, one that differs strongly will be investigated in order to build up, through the process of contrast, interpretative hypotheses, and also to ensure that the full scope of the field of investigation is being considered. The two principles of contrast may be connected to one another with regard to the processes for the reconstruction of different discourses within a discursive field, and they are applied until the point where the material has been exhaustively analyzed and there are no further results with regard to the research questions. In this way, individual discourses – analogously to the process of type-formation – may on the one hand be characterized as precisely as possible, and on the other hand the overall spectrum of the field, that is, the total number of available discourses, may be recorded. Individual analyses are repeatedly interrupted by moments of hypothesis-formation and are gradually consolidated into the form of 'discourses': the interpreter will inevitably carry out the stylizing attributions necessary to achieve results. In this, abstractions will increasingly be made from the starting material. The results are of an idealized character insofar as they diverge to a greater or lesser extent from the actual discourse fragments.

The gradual detailed analysis of a range of data implies that decisions must be made about whether a document or sections of it may be attributed to one specific discourse or to another. From this analysis as complete a configuration as possible of phenomenal structure can be assembled; this makes it possible to record the limited number of important meaning patterns (frames, interpretative schemes) that are communicated in a discourse. It can also make clear referential relationships between documents, and so on. It is possible, therefore, to derive partial components of a complete discourse from every analyzed document, from some documents more fully, and from others rather less. Therefore, only if components of different individual documents can be attributed, in the course of the analysis, to one single discourse, then it is possible to reconstruct the whole particular content structure of such a discourse. A helpful concept in the preparation and presentation of the discourse-related results of detailed analyses is the concept of *interpretative repertoires*, suggested by Jonathan Potter and Margaret Wetherell, which we mentioned in Chapter 3 (above). The analysis of formal and rhetorical structures, phenomenal structures, meaning patterns and their narrative links may be summarized in the representation of this kind of discourse-specific *interpretative repertoire*. It contains the typified and typical constituents that are used within a discourse 'for the interpretation of actions, of one's own person and of social structures while speaking' (Potter and Wetherell 1998: 145). Apart from the meaning patterns, these also include the surface structures of utterances, for example frequently used images (metaphors), typical narrative patterns or cognitive structures (such as classifications). These elements of a discourse are linked in a specific way by a kind of meta-narrative, an overall storyline in the discourse. Other possibilities for representation or consolidation of the results of individual analyses that have hitherto scarcely been used in discourse research consist of graphic or tabular representations, for instance concerning constellations of actors (or discourse coalitions) within a discursive field or for the visual representation of reconstructed relationships and processes in a particular field.[2]

The results of the different steps – that is, of the interpretative analysis, the analysis of the situated nature and material form, and the consideration of the formal and linguistic-rhetorical elements – are then inter-related, so long as this is important for the research questions. Finally the results of the detailed analysis are placed in a further interpretative context – for example, questions of power or hegemony, the role of individual actors and events in the discourse or discursive field, and so on. This is equally true for the answering of questions about the possible causes, background conditions and effects of specific discursive sequences. To put this more generally, it

---

[2]On this point see, for example, Keller (1998: 265ff, 2012); Clarke (2005).

is therefore a question of interrelating the results of the data analysis with knowledge of contexts, social processes and other factors, insofar as this is required by the questions under investigation.

The quality and validity of the results of the analysis, i.e. questions of research validity and reliability, are in this context – as everywhere in qualitative social research – difficult to judge, and in the strict form of quantitative social research they are certainly not suitable for use as a standard measure (see, in general terms, Flick 2009: 383ff). Illustration using selected textual examples and specially prepared analyses of sample cases can do no more than attenuate this problem. Orientational aids for discourse research are to be found in different reflections on specific 'soft' criteria in qualitative social research, focusing particularly on the consistency of the procedural context of questions, data collection, analysis and overall interpretation (on this see the helpful ideas in Flick 2009: 381ff). Undoubtedly, the different methodological approaches to texts (explained above) may be 'practised' more or less rigorously; this, of course, does not constitute a guarantee of creativity, flashes of insight and hypothesis-formation. In the context of the meaning-pattern analysis mentioned above, the use of interpretative groups – who have to agree via argumentation on a common interpretation of textual passages – aims at an appropriate validity for the statement thus achieved. In the culturalist discourse research of Gamson and others (see Chapter 2.5), the step of quantitative data analysis relies on the strategies used elsewhere in quantitative social research: for example training of interviewers, comparison of coding and so on. As Guilhaumou (2006) noted, it should once again be remembered that appropriate conventionalizations should not be overstated. An investigation may ultimately also be considered as convincing, surprising, innovative or stimulating even if it does not adhere to the usual criteria, but seeks out and discovers new ways and makes them accessible to others.

6.2 Interpretation and Presentation of Results

After the stages of detailed analysis and their aggregation into general discourse-related statements there remain for discourse researchers two more tasks that concern every kind of empirical investigation: on the one hand there is the stage of the interpretation and balancing of empirical results with regard to the questions that have been pursued in the investigation and, in the course of it, have perhaps been greatly modified. On the other hand there is the question of balancing, of relations to and involvement in the more general social science discourse context, whether it be discourse research or the object area being investigated. What is helpful here is the use of the notes, memos and commentaries that have been made in the course of the investigation. Another useful strategy is the free associative development of ideas and hypotheses, their repeated presentation, reformulation and discussion with others and in front of an audience.

Guidelines for the Interpretation of the Overall Results

- How has the original research question changed in the course of the investigation?
- What results were achieved with regard to the research questions?
- What, therefore, in summary form, are the reconstructed features of a discourse or a discursive field, the rules of formation, the discourse strategies, and so on?
- How do socio-historical context, discursive fields, discourses, practices and *dispositifs* relate to one another?
- What explanations can be formulated for the reconstructed structuration processes of and through discourses?
- In what relation are the results to other perspectives and statements on the same or similar research objects? Are the results refuted, complemented or confirmed by these other interpretations?
- what can be gained from the investigative process for the discourse-theory perspective, for methodological procedures in discourse research, and so on?
- What contribution do the results make to social science knowledge and discussion of the object area?

In the presentation of results, discourse research has hitherto been text-heavy, dominated by a sequence of narrative text passages, which formulate results in continuous text and support them with inbuilt textual evidence (citations). Apart from tabular treatment of the reconstructed elements of discourses, graphic representations have hardly been used (see figure below). Here there is certainly a need for experimental representations. In principle, the presentation of results is faced with the same problem or dilemma as all forms of (qualitative) social research: it is, of course, true that sample analytical

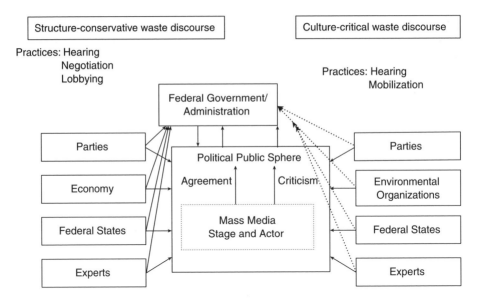

Structure-conservative waste discourse

Culture-critical waste discourse

Practices: Hearing
            Negotiation
            Lobbying

Practices: Hearing
            Mobilization

Federal Government/
Administration

Parties

Political Public Sphere

Parties

Economy

Agreement

Criticism

Environmental
Organizations

Federal States

Mass Media
Stage and Actor

Federal States

Experts

Experts

Figure   Example for mapping. The public space of waste discourse in the Federal
             Republic of Germany: the media as an arena of conflict.[1]
             Solid arrows indicate direct access/strong influence; dotted arrows indicate
             indirect/weak access.

procedures on utterance units can and perhaps should be presented, so that the analytical process itself becomes intelligible and also transparent, within the limits of possibility. But the overall process of reconstruction as such, can not be represented visually or as text, because of the fundamental impossibility of fixing it in writing. This is much the same for the phases of generating ideas, drawing conclusions, and formulating and testing hypotheses. For this reason it is possible to explain and illustrate the procedure using individual data extracts, but in general terms it is scarcely possible to avoid the fact that data samples have an illustrative character in the presentation of results. Ultimately the more or less *successfully communicated* credibility and sincerity of the researchers will influence the reception of an investigation. And this problem is not unique to discourse research.

---

[1]Figure adapted from Keller (1998: 265). See, in contrast, the structure of the French debate on waste and the additional representations (ibid: 261ff). See Keller (2011b, 2012) and Clarke (2005) for further possibilites.

SEVEN

Concluding Remarks

The preceding chapters have introduced and explained, in a condensed form, the steps in the methodological procedure of a social science or sociology-of-knowledge investigation of discourse. I would like to emphasize once again that these should be understood as proposals and stimuli and not at all as prescriptions and obstacles to the investigators' own creativity. They require, therefore, adjustment in accordance with the investigators' own research questions and theoretical perspectives. Creativity in the research process is indispensable for the further development and, more particularly, for the social science potential of discourse research. In our discussion of the separate stages we suggested, in different ways, the locations where deficits in Discourse Analysis may be identified. This undoubtedly concerns the interfaces between Discourse Analysis and discourse theory or discourse research; these also include the treatments to which we have alluded of other data formats apart from texts and of methods of analysing them. These ultimately also include experiments in the processing of results. The danger of making false and oversimplified conclusions from 'the discourse' to 'the practice' should be avoided. In discourse research this will be successful to the extent that it examines the material side of discourses both in respect of discourse production and in terms of discourse reception and discourse effects. Therefore it should develop an appropriate description of the role of social actors in discourses, acknowledge the socio-historical contexts of discourses and place its results in relation to other theoretical and research perspectives in the social sciences. For even though there are many arguments in favour of discourse research, it should not be forgotten that reality and society are complex phenomena, which *by their very nature* not only permit, but even require, different modes of approach within the social sciences – for example, social structure analyses, the investigation of unintended consequences, and theories of structuration.

Bibliography

Althusser, L. (2001) 'Ideology and Ideological State Apparatuses'. In: Althusser, L.: *Lenin and Philosophy and other essays*. New York and London 85–126 [1970].

Andersen, N. A. (2003) *Discursive Analytical Strategies. Understanding Foucault, Koselleck, Laclau, Luhmann*. Bristol.

Angermüller, J. (2007) *Nach dem Strukturalismus. Theoriediskurs und intellektuelles Feld in Frankreich*. Bielefeld.

Angermüller, J., and van Dyk, S. (Eds.) (2010) *Diskursanalyse meets Gouvernement-alitätsforschung*. Frankfurt/Main.

Barker, C. (2000) *Cultural Studies*. London.

Barker, C. and Galasinski, D. (2001) *Cultural Studies and Discourse Analysis*. London.

Barthes, R. (1967) *Elements of Semiology*. New York.

Bateman, J. (2008) *Multimodality and Genre. A Foundation for the Systematic Analysis of Multimodal Documents*. Hampshire/New York.

Bätschmann, O. (2001) *Einführung in die kunstgeschichtliche Hermeneutik*. Darmstadt.

Bechmann, S. (2007) *Gesundheitssemantiken der Moderne. Eine Diskursanalyse der Debatten über die Reform der Krankenversicherung*. Berlin.

Becker-Schmidt, R. and Knapp G.-A. (2000) *Feministische Theorien zur Einführung*. Hamburg.

Berger, P. L. and Luckmann, Th. (1975) *The Social Construction of Reality. A Treatise in the Sociology of Knowledge*. Harmondsworth [1966].

Bergmann, J. (2004) 'Conversation Analysis'. In: Flick, U., Kardorff, E. von and Steinke, I. (Eds.) (2004) *A Companion to Qualitative Research*. London, 296–302.

Billig, M. (1996) *Arguing and thinking*. Cambridge.

Billig, M. and Schegloff, E. A. (1999) 'Critical Discourse Analysis and Conversation Analysis: an Exchange between Michael Billig and Emanuel A. Schegloff'. In: *Discourse and Society* 10 (4), 543–582.

Bödeker, H. E. (Ed.) (2002) *Begriffsgeschichte, Diskursgeschichte, Metapherngeschichte*. Göttingen.

Bogdal, K.-M. (1999) *Historische Diskursanalyse der Literatur*. Opladen.

Bohnsack, R. (1999) *Rekonstruktive Sozialforschung*. Opladen.

Bohnsack, R. (2008) *Qualitative Bild- und Videointerpretation: Die dokumentarische Methode*. München.

Bormann, Inka (2009) *Zwischenräume der Veränderung. Innovationen und ihr Transfer im Feld von Bildung und Erziehung. Habilitationsschrift.* Berlin: Freie Universität Berlin.

Bourdieu, P. (1984) *Distinction: A Social Critique of the Judgement of Taste.* Cambridge.

Bourdieu, P. (1990a) *The Logic of Practice.* Stanford [1980].

Bourdieu, P. (1990b) *In Other Words. Essays Towards a Reflexive Sociology.* Stanford.

Bourdieu, P. (1992) *Language and Symbolic Power.* Oxford.

Bourdieu, P. and Boltanski, L. (2008) *La production de l'idéologie dominante.* Paris [1976].

Bowker, G. C. and Leigh Star, S.L. (2000) *Sorting things out.* Cambridge.

Brand, K.-W., Eder, K. and Poferl, A. (Eds.) (1997) *Ökologische Kommunikation in Deutschland.* Opladen.

Breckner, R. (2010) *Sozialtheorie des Bildes. Zur interpretativen Analyse von Bildern und Fotografien.* Bielefeld.

Bröckling, U. (2007) *Das unternehmerische Selbst.* Frankfurt/Main.

Bröckling, U., Krasmann, S. and Lemke, T. (Eds.) (2000) *Gouvernementalität der Gegenwart.* Frankfurt/Main.

Brown, G. and Yule, G. (1983) *Discourse Analysis.* Cambridge.

Brunner, C. (2010) *Wissensobjekt Selbstmordattentat.* Wiesbaden.

Brünner, G. and Graefen, G. (1994) *Texte und Diskurse. Methoden und Forschungsergebnisse der Funktionalen Pragmatik.* Opladen.

Brünner, G., Fiehler, R. and Kindt, W. (Eds.) (1999) *Angewandte Diskursforschung*, 2 Vol. Opladen.

Bublitz, H. (Ed.) (1998) *Das Geschlecht der Moderne.* Frankfurt/Main.

Bublitz, H. (1999) *Foucaults Archäologie des kulturellen Unbewußten.* Frankfurt/Main.

Bublitz, H. (2003) *Diskurs.* Bielefeld.

Bublitz, H. (2011) 'Differenz und Integration. Zur diskursanalytischen Rekonstruktion der Regelstrukturen sozialer Wirklichkeit'. In: Keller, R., Hirseland, A., Schneider, W. and Viehöver, W. (Eds.) (2011) *Handbuch Sozialwissenschaftliche Diskursanalyse Vol. 1: Theorien und Methoden.* 3. Ed. Wiesbaden [2001], 227–262.

Bublitz, H., Bührmann, A. D., Hanke, C. and Seier, A. (Eds.) (1999) *Das Wuchern der Diskurse. Perspektiven der Diskursanalyse Foucaults.* Frankfurt/Main.

Bublitz, H., Hanke, C. and Seier, A. (2000) *Der Gesellschaftskörper. Zur Neuordnung von Kultur und Geschlecht um 1900.* Frankfurt/Main.

Bührmann, A. D. (1995) *Das authentische Geschlecht. Die Sexualitätsdebatte der Neuen Frauenbewegung und die Foucaultsche Machtanalyse.* Münster.

Bührmann, A., Diaz-Bone, R., Gutiérrez-Rodríguez, E., Schneider, W., Kendall, G. and Tirado, R. (Eds.) (2007) 'From Michel Foucault's Theory of Discourse to Empirical Discourse Research'. In: *Forum Qualitative Sozialforschung / Forum: Qualitative Social Research*, Vol 8, No 2 [http://www.qualitative-research.net/index.php/fqs/issue/view/7; 13.3.2012]

Bührmann, A. and Schneider, W. (2008) *Vom Diskurs zum Dispositiv.* Bielefeld.

Burchell, G., Gordon, C. and Miller, P. (Eds.) (1991) *The Foucault Effect*. Hertfordshire.

Burke, K. (1945) *A Grammar of Motives*. New York.

Burr, V. (1997) *An Introduction to Social Constructionism*. London.

Burri, R. V. (2008) 'Bilder als soziale Praxis: Grundlegungen einer Soziologie des Visuellen'. In: *Zeitschrift für Soziologie* 37 (4) 342–358.

Busse, D. (1987) *Historische Semantik. Analyse eines Programms*. Stuttgart.

Busse, D. (2008) 'Diskurslinguistik als Epistemologie. Das verstehensrelevante Wissen als Gegenstand linguistischer Forschung'. In: Warnke, I. and Spitzmüller, J. (Eds.) (2008) *Methoden der Diskurslinguistik. Sprachwissenschaftliche Zugänge zur transtextuellen Ebene*. Berlin, 57–88.

Busse, D., Hermanns, F. and Teubert, W. (Eds.) (1994) *Begriffsgeschichte und Diskursgeschichte*. Opladen.

Busse, D., Niehr, Th. and Wengeler, M. (Eds.) (2005) *Brisante Semantik. Neuere Konzepte und Forschungsergebnisse einer kulturwissenschaftlichen Linguistik*. Tübingen.

Busse, D., Teubert, W. (1994) 'Ist Diskurs ein sprachwissenschaftliches Objekt?' In: Busse, D., Hermanns, F. and Teubert, W. (Eds.) (1994) *Begriffsgeschichte und Diskursgeschichte*. Opladen, 10–28.

Butler, J. (1990) *Gender Trouble*. New York.

Butler, J. (1993) *Bodies that Matter*. New York.

Cameron, D. (2001) *Working with Spoken Discourse*. London.

Carabine, J. (2001) 'Unmarried Motherhood 1830–1990: A Genealogical Analysis'. In: Wetherell, M., Taylor, S. and Yates, S. J. (Eds.), (2001b) *Discourse as Data*. London, 267–310.

Chandler, D. (2002) *Semiotics: The Basics*. London.

Charaudeau, P. and Maingueneau, D. (Eds.) (2002) *Dictionnaire d'Analyse du Discours*. Paris.

Chartier, R. (1989) *Cultural History: Between Practices and Representations*. Ithaca.

Chartier, R. (1992) *Die unvollendete Vergangenheit*. Frankfurt/Main.

Chilton, P. A. and Schaffner, C. (Eds.) (2002) *Politics as Talk and Text*. London.

Chouliaraki, L. and Fairclough, N. (1999) *Discourse in Late Modernity*. Edinburgh.

Christmann, G. (forthcoming) *Towards a communicative construction of spaces*. Papers of the International Conference at IRS Erkner, June 2010 [in preparation].

Christmann, G. B. (2004) *Dresdens Glanz, Stolz der Dresdner. Lokale Kommunikation, Stadtkultur und städtische Identität*. Wiesbaden.

Clarke, A. (2005) *Situational Analysis*. London.

Corbin, J. and Strauss, A. (2008) *Basics of Qualitative Research*. London.

Danaher, G., Schirato, T. and Webb, J. (2000) *Understanding Foucault*. London.

D'Andrade, R. (1995) *The Development of Cognitive Anthropology*. Cambridge.

Darier, E. (Ed.) (1999) *Discourses of the Environment*. Oxford.

Dean, M. (1999) *Governmentality*. London.

Deleuze, G. (1988) *Foucault*. Minneapolis/London.

Demirovic, A. (1988). 'Ideologie, Diskurs und Hegemonie'. In: *Zeitschrift für Semiotik* 1/2 (10), 63–74.

Demirovic, A. and Prigge, W. (Eds.) (1988) *Diskurs – Macht – Hegemonie. Themenschwerpunkt der kultuRRevolution 17/18.*

Denzin, N. K. (2004) 'Reading Film'. In: Flick, U., Kardorff, E. v. and Steinke, I. (Eds.) (2004) *A Companion to Qualitative Research*. London, 237–247.

Deppermann, A. (2008) *Gespräche analysieren*. 4th edn. Wiesbaden

Diaz-Bone, R. (2006a) 'Operative Anschlüsse: Zur Entstehung der Foucaultschen Diskursanalyse in der Bundesrepublik'. Jürgen Link im Gespräch mit Rainer Diaz-Bone. In: *Forum Qualitative Sozialforschung* [Online Journal], 7 (3), Art. 20.; www.qualitative-research.net/fqs-texte/3-06/06-3-20-d.htm [15.5.2006]

Diaz-Bone, R. (2006b) 'Kritische Diskursanalyse: Zur Ausarbeitung einer problembezogenen Diskursanalyse im Anschluss an Foucault'. Siegfried Jäger im Gespräch mit Rainer Diaz-Bone. In: *Forum Qualitative Sozialforschung* [Online Journal], 7 (3), Art. 21; www.qualitative-research.net/fqs-texte/3-06/06-3-20-d.htm [15.5.2006]

Diaz-Bone, R. (2008) *Kulturwelt, Diskurs und Lebensstil*. 2. ed. Wiesbaden.

Diaz-Bone, R. (2010) 'Was ist der Beitrag der Diskurslinguistik für die Foucaultsche Diskursanalyse'. In: *Forum Qualitative Sozialforschung/Forum: Qualitative Social Research* [Online Journal], 11 (2), Art. 19; http://www.qualitative-research.net/index.php/fqs/article/view/1454/2955.

Diaz-Bone, R. and Krell, G. (Eds.) (2010) *Diskurs und Ökonomie. Diskursanalytische Perspektiven auf Märkte und Organisationen*. Wiesbaden.

Diaz-Bone, R. and Schneider, W. (2010) 'Qualitative Datenanalysesoftware in der sozialwissenschaftlichen Diskursanalyse'. In: Keller, R., Hirseland, A., Schneider, W. and Viehöver, W. (Eds.) (2010) *Handbuch Sozialwissenschaftliche Diskursanalyse Vol. 2: Forschungspraxis*. 4. Ed. Wiesbaden [2003], 491–530.

Diekmannshenke, H., Klemm, M. and Stöckl, H. (Eds.) (2010) *Bildlinguistik*. Berlin.

Dijk, T. van (Ed.) (1985) *Handbook of Discourse Analysis*, 4 Vol. London.

Dijk, T. van (1988) *News as Discourse*. Hillsdale

Dijk, T. van (1993) 'Principles of Critical Discourse Analysis'. In: *Discourse and Society* 4, 249–283.

Dijk, T. van (Ed.) (1997a) *Discourse as Structure and Process. Discourse Studies*, Vol. 1. London.

Dijk, T. van (Ed.) (1997b) *Discourse as Social Interaction. Discourse Studies*, Vol. 2. London.

Dijk, T. van (1997c) 'The Study of Discourse'. In: Dijk, T. van (Ed.) (1997a) *Discourse as Structure and Process. Discourse Studies*, Vol. 1. London, 1–34.

Dijk, T. van (1998) *Ideology – A Multidisciplinary Approach*. London.

Dijk, T. (van 2008a) *Discourse and Context. A Sociocognitive Approach*. Cambridge.

Dijk, T. van (2008b) *Society and Discourse: How Social Contexts Influence Text and Talk*. Cambridge.

Donati, P. R. (2011) 'Die Rahmenanalyse politischer Diskurse'. In: Keller, R., Hirseland, A., Schneider, W. and Viehöver,W. (Eds.) (2011) *Handbuch Sozialwissenschaftliche Diskursanalyse Vol. 1: Theorien und Methoden*. 3. Ed. Wiesbaden [2001], 147–178.

Dosse, F. (1997) *History of Structuralism. Volume II. The Sign Sets 1967–Present*. Minneapolis/London.

Dosse, F. (1998a) *History of Structuralism. Volume I. The Rising Sign 1945–1966*. Minneapolis/London.

Dosse, F. (1998b) *Empire Of Meaning. The Humanization Of The Social Sciences*. Minneapolis/London.

Dreyfus, H. and Rabinow, P. (1982) *Michel Foucault. Beyond Structuralism and Hermeneutics*. Chicago.

Duden, B. (1991) *Der Frauenleib als öffentlicher Ort*. Hamburg [eng. Translation: *Disembodying Women: Perspectives on Pregnancy and the Unborn*. Harvard, 1993].

During, S. (2005) *Cultural Studies: A Critical Introduction*. London.

Dyk, S. van (2006) *Die Ordnung des Konsenses*. Berlin.

Eberle, T. S. (1997) 'Ethnomethodologische Konversationsanalyse'. In: Hitzler, R. and Honer, A. (Eds.) *Sozialwissenschaftliche Hermeneutik*. München, 245–280.

Eco, U. (1978) *A Theory of Semiotics*. Bloomington.

Eco, U. (1991) *The Limits of Interpretation*. Bloomington.

Eder, F. (Ed.) (2006) *Historische Diskursanalysen. Genealogie, Theorie, Anwendungen*. Wiesbaden.

Edwards, D. (1997) *Discourse and Cognition*. London.

Edwards, D. and Potter, J. (1992) *Discursive Psychology*. London.

Ehlich, K. (Ed.) (1994) *Diskursanalyse in Europa*. Frankfurt/Main.

Eribon, D. (1992) *Michel Foucault*. London.

Fairclough, N. (1989) *Language and Power*. London.

Fairclough, N. (1992) *Critical Language Awareness*. London.

Fairclough, N. (1995) *Critical Discourse Analysis*. London.

Fairclough, N. (1998) *Discourse and Social Change*. Cambridge.

Fairclough, N. (2003) *Analysing Discourse: A Social and Critical Approach*. London.

Fairclough, N. (2011) 'Globaler Kapitalismus und kritisches Diskursbewusstsein'. In: Keller, R., Hirseland, A., Schneider, W. and Viehöver, W. (Eds.) (2011) *Handbuch Sozialwissenschaftliche Diskursanalyse Vol. 1: Theorien und Methoden*. 3. Ed. Wiesbaden [2001], 339–356.

Fairclough, I. and Fairclough, N. (2012) *Political Discourse Analysis: A Method for Advanced Students*. Oxford.

Fairclough, N. and Wodak, R. (1997) 'Critical Discourse Analysis'. In: Van Dijk, T. (Ed.) (1997b), *Discourse as Social Interaction. Discourse Studies, Vol. 2*. London, 258–284.

Faulstich, W. (1988) *Die Filminterpretation*. Göttingen.

Felder, E. (Ed.) (2009) *Sprache*. Heidelberg.

Felder, E. and Müller, M. (Eds.) (2008) *Wissen durch Sprache. Theorie, Praxis und Erkenntnisinteresse des Forschungsznetzwerkes, 'Sprache und Wissen'.* Heidelberg.

Ferree, M. M., Gamson, W., Gerhards, J. and Rucht, D. (2002) *Shaping Abortion Discourse: Democracy and The Public Sphere in Germany and the United States.* New York.

Finlayson, G. (2005) *Habermas: A Very Short Introduction.* Oxford.

Fischer, F. and Forester, J. (1993) *The Argumentative Turn in Policy Analysis and Planning.* Durham.

Fischer, F. and Gottweis, H. (Eds.) (2012) *The Argumentative Turn Revisited: Public Policy as Communicative Practice.* Durham.

Flick, U. (2009) *An Introduction to Qualitative Research.* 4th Ed. London.

Flick, U., Kardorff, E. von, and Steinke, I. (Eds.) (2004) *A Companion to Qualitative Research.* London.

Fohrmann, J. and Müller, H. (Eds.) (1988) *Diskurstheorien und Literaturwissenschaft.* Frankfurt/Main.

Foucault, M. (1977a) *Discipline and Punish.* New York [1975].

Foucault, M. (1977b) 'Nietzsche, Genealogy, History'. In: Foucault, M. (1977) *Language, Counter-Memory, Practice. Selected Essays.* New York, 139–164.

Foucault, M. (1988–1990) *History of Sexuality*, 3 volumes. New York.

Foucault, M. (1988a) *Madness and Civilization. A History of Insanity in the Age of Reason.* New York [1961].

Foucault, M. (1988b) *Power/Knowledge: Selected Interviews and Other Writings, 1972–1977.* New York.

Foucault, M. (1991a) 'Politics and the Study of Discourse'. In: Burchell, G., Gordon, C. and Miller, P. (Eds.) (1991) *The Foucault Effect.* Hertfordshire, 53–72.

Foucault, M. (1991b) 'Questions of Method'. In: Burchell, G., Gordon, C. and Miller, P. (Eds.) *The Foucault Effect.* Hertfordshire, 73–86.

Foucault, M. (1991c) *The Order of Things. An Archeology of the Human Sciences.* London [1966].

Foucault, M. (1992) *The Use of Pleasure. The History of Sexuality: Vol. 2.* London [1984].

Foucault, M. (1994) *The Birth of the Clinic. An Archaeology of Medical Perception.* New York [1963].

Foucault, M. (1998) *The Will to Knowledge. History of Sexuality: Vol. 1.* London [1976].

Foucault, M. (2001) *Schriften in vier Bänden. Dits et Écrits, Vol. 1: 1954–1969.* Ed. von D. Defert u. F. Ewald. Frankfurt/Main.

Foucault, M. (2002) *Schriften in vier Bänden. Dits et Écrits, Vol. 2: 1976–1979.* Ed. von D. Defert u. F. Ewald. Frankfurt/Main.

Foucault, M. (2003) *Schriften in vier Bänden. Dits et Écrits, Vol. 3: 1980–1988.* Ed. von D. Defert u. F. Ewald. Frankfurt/Main.

Foucault, M. (2005) *Schriften in vier Bänden. Dits et Écrits, Vol. 4: 1970–1975.* Ed. von D. Defert u. F. Ewald. Frankfurt/Main.

Foucault, M. (2010) *The Archeology of Knowledge and The Discourse on Language*. New York (following the first translation 1972 by Tavistock Publ.) [1969; 1971].

Fox, N. J. (1998) 'Foucault, Foucauldians and sociology'. In *British Journal of Sociology* 49 (3), 415–433.

Freitag, W. (2005) *Contergan. Eine genealogische Studie des Zusammenhangs wissenschaftlicher Diskurse und biographischer Erfahrungen*. Münster.

Fritz, G., and Hundsnurscher, F. (Eds.) (1994) *Handbuch der Dialoganalyse*. Tübingen.

Gamson, W. A. (1988a) 'Political Discourse and Collective Action'. In *International Social Movement Research*, Vol. 1. London, 219–244.

Gamson, W. A. (1988b) 'The 1987 Distinguished Lecture: A Constructionist Approach to Mass Media and Public Opinion'. In *Symbolic Interaction* 2, 161–174.

Gamson, W. A. and Lasch, K. E. (1983) 'The political culture of social welfare policy'. In: Spiro, S. E. and Yuchtman-Yaar, E. (Eds.) *Evaluating the Welfare State*. New York, 397–415.

Gamson, W. A. and Modigliani, A. (1987) 'The changing culture of affirmative action'. In: Braungart, R. D. and Braungart, M. M. (Eds.) *Research in Political Sociology*, Vol. 3. Greenwich, 137–177.

Gamson, W. A. and Modigliani, A. (1989) 'Media discourse and public opinion on nuclear power: a constructionist approach'. In *American Journal of Sociology* 95, 1–37.

Gamson, W. A. and Stuart, D. (1992) 'Media discourse as a symbolic contest: The bomb in political cartoons'. In *Sociological Forum* 7, 55–86.

Gamson, W. A., Croteau, D., Hoynes, W. and Sasson, T. (1992) 'Media Images and the Social Construction of Reality'. In *Annual Review of Sociology* 18, 373–393.

Gandhi, L. (1998) *Postcolonial Theory. A Critical Introduction*. Edinburgh.

Garfinkel, H. (1967) *Studies in Ethnomethodology*. Englewood Cliffs.

Gee, J. P. (1999) *An Introduction to Discourse Analysis: Theory and Method*. London.

Gee, J. P. (2010) *How to do Discourse Analysis: A Toolkit*. London.

Gee, J., Hull, G. and Lankshear, C. (1996) *The New Work Order*. London.

Geertz, C. (1973) *The Interpretation of Cultures*. New York.

Gergen, K. J. (1999) *An Invitation to Social Constructionism*. London.

Gerhards, J. (1992) 'Dimensionen und Strategien öffentlicher Diskurse'. In: *Journal für Sozialforschung* 32 (3/4), 307–318.

Gerhards, J. (2010) 'Diskursanalyse als systematische Inhaltsanalyse'. In: Keller, R., Hirseland, A., Schneider, W. and Viehöver, W. (Eds.) (2010b) *Handbuch Sozialwissenschaftliche Diskursanalyse Vol. 2: Forschungspraxis. 4. Ed.* Wiesbaden [2003], 299–324.

Gerhards, J. and Schäfer, M. S. (2006) *Die Herstellung einer öffentlichen Hegemonie. Humangenomforschung in der deutschen und der US-amerikanischen Presse*. Wiesbaden.

Giddens, A. (1986) *The Constitution of Society. Outline of the Theory of Structuration*. Berkeley.

Giddens, A. (1991) *The Consequences of Modernity*. Stanford.

Glaser, B. (1978) *Theoretical Sensitivity*. Mill Valley.

Glaser, B. and Strauss, A. (1967) *The Discovering of Grounded Theory*. Chicago.

Glasze, G. and Mattissek, A. (Eds.) (2009) *Handbuch Diskurs und Raum: Theorien und Methoden für die Humangeographie sowie die sozial- und kulturwissenschaftliche Raumforschung*. Bielefeld.

Goffman, E. (1974) *Frame Analysis: An Essay on the Organization of Experience*. New York.

Gottschalk-Mazouz, N. (2000) *Diskursethik*. Berlin.

Gottweis, H. (1998) *Governing Molecules: The Discursive Politics of Genetic Engineering in Europe and the United States*. Cambridge.

Gramsci, A. (2010/2011) *Prison Notebooks. Vol.1,2,3*. New York [1929–1937].

Grenfell, M. (Ed.) (2008) *Pierre Bourdieu. Key Concepts*. Durham.

Grochla, N. (2008) *Qualität und Bildung: Eine Analyse des wissenschaftlichen Diskurses in der Frühpädagogik*. Münster.

Guilhaumou, J. (1989) *Sprache und Politik in der Französischen Revolution*. Frankfurt/Main.

Guilhaumou, J. (2006) *Discours et Événement. L'histoire Langagière des Concepts*. Besançon.

Guilhaumou, J. (2010) 'Geschichte und Sprachwissenschaft'. In: Keller, R., Hirseland, A., Schneider, W. and Viehöver, W. (Ed.) (2010) *Handbuch Sozialwissenschaftliche Diskursanalyse Vol. 2: Forschungspraxis*. 4. Ed. Wiesbaden [2003], 19–66.

Gusfield, J. (1981) *The Culture of Public Problems*. Chicago.

Gusfield, J. (1989) 'Introduction'. In: Burke, K. (Ed.) *On Symbols and Society*. Chicago, 1–49.

Gusfield, J. (1996) *Contested Meanings*. Madison.

Habermas, J. (1985) *The Theory of Communicative Action*, 2 Volumes. Boston.

Habermas, J. (1991a) 'Discourse Ethics: Notes on a Program of Philosophical Justification'. In Habermas, J. (1991) *Moral Consciousness and Communicative Action*. Cambridge, 43–115.

Habermas, J. (1997) *Between Facts and Norms. Contributions to a Discourse Theory of Law and Democracy*. Cambridge.

Hacking, I. (2000) *The Social Construction of What?* Harvard.

Hajer, M. A. (1995) *The Politics of Environmental Discourse*. Oxford.

Hajer, M. A. (2002) 'Discourse Analysis and the Study of Policy Making'. In *European Political Science* Vol. 2, Nr. 1 [Online-Journal: www.essex.ac.uk/ecpr/publications/eps/onlineisssues/autumn2002; 29.7.2003]

Hajer, M. A. (2010) 'Argumentative Diskursanalyse'. In: Keller, R., Hirseland, A., Schneider, W. and Viehöver, W. (Eds.) (2010) *Handbuch Sozialwissenschaftliche Diskursanalyse Vol. 2: Forschungspraxis*. 4. Ed. Wiesbaden [2003], 271–298.

Hall, S. (1980) 'Cultural studies: two paradigms'. In *Media Culture & Society* Volume 2, Number 1, 57–72.

Hall, S. (1991) 'Signification, Representation, Ideology: Althusser and the Post-Structuralist Debates'. In: Avery, R. K. and Eason, D. (Eds.) *Critical Studies in Mass Communication*. New York, 88–113.

Hall, S. (1997) *Representation: Cultural Representations and Signifying Practices*. London.

Hampsher-Monk, I. (1984) 'Review Article: Political Languages in Time – The Work of J. G. A. Pocock'. In *British Journal of Political Science* 14 (1), 89–116.

Hampsher-Monk, I., Tilmans, K. and van Vree, F. (1998) *History of Concepts. Comparative Perspectives*. Amsterdam.

Hark, S. (2005) *Dissidente Partizipation. Eine Diskursgeschichte des Feminismus*. Frankfurt/Main.

Hark, S. (2011) 'Feministische Theorie – Diskurs – Dekonstruktion'. In: Keller, R., Hirseland, A., Schneider, W. and Viehöver, W. (Eds.) (2011) *Handbuch Sozialwissen schaftliche Diskursanalyse Vol. 1: Theorien und Methoden*. 3. Ed. Wiesbaden [2001], 357–377.

Harper, D. (2004) 'Photography as Social Science Data'. In: Flick, U., Kardorff, E. v. and Steinke, I. (Eds.) (2004) *A Companion to Qualitative Research*. London, 231–236.

Harris, Z. S. (1952) 'Discourse Analysis'. In: *Language* 28 (1), 1–30.

Hekman, S. J. (Ed.) (1996) *Feminist Interpretations of Michel Foucault*. Pennsylvania.

Helsloot, N. and Hak, T. (2007) Pêcheux's Contribution to Discourse Analysis [47 par-agraphs]. In: *Forum Qualitative Sozialforschung / Forum: Qualitative Social Research*, 8(2), Art. 1, http://nbn-resolving.de/urn:nbn:de:0114-fqs070218 [15.3.2012]

Hepp, A. (1999) *Cultural Studies und Medienanalyse*. Opladen.

Hepp, A. and Winter, R. (Eds.) (1999) *Kultur – Macht – Medien*. Opladen.

Hermanns, F. (1994) 'Linguistische Anthropologie'. In: Busse, D., Hermanns, F. and Teubert, W. (Eds.) (1994) *Begriffsgeschichte und Diskursgeschichte*. Opladen, 29–59.

Hermanns, F. (1995) 'Sprachgeschichte als Mentalitätsgeschichte'. In: Gardt, A., Mattheier, K. and Reichmann, O. (Eds.) (1995) *Sprachgeschichte des Neuhochdeutschen*. Tübingen, 69–101.

Hermanns, F. (2007) 'Diskurshermeneutik'. In: Warnke, I. (2007) *Diskurslinguistik nach Foucault. Theorie und Gegenstände*. Berlin, 187–210.

Hickethier, K. (2001) *Film- und Fernsehanalyse*. Stuttgart.

Hirschauer, S. and Amann, K. (1997) *Die Befremdung der eigenen Kultur*. Frankfurt/Main

Hitzler, R. (1994) 'Sinnbasteln'. In: Mörth, I. and Fröhlich, G. (Eds.) (1994) *Das symbolische Kapital der Lebensstile*. Frankfurt/Main, 75–92.

Hitzler, R. (2000) 'Sinnrekonstruktion'. In: *Schweizerische Zeitschrift für Soziologie* 26 (3), 459–484.

Hitzler, R. and Honer, A. (Eds.) (1997) *Sozialwissenschaftliche Hermeneutik*. Opladen.

Hitzler, R. and Honer, A. (2002) 'Qualitative Methoden'. In: Nohlen, D. and Schultze, R.-O. (Eds.) *Lexikon der Politikwissenschaft*. Vol. 2. München, 755–759.

Hitzler, R., Reichertz, J. and Schröer, N. (Eds.) (1999a) *Hermeneutische Wissenssoziologie*. Konstanz.

Hitzler, R., Reichertz, J. and Schröer, N. (1999b) 'Das Arbeitsfeld einer hermeneutischen Wissenssoziologie'. In: Hitzler, R., Reichertz, J. and Schröer, N. (Eds.) (1999a) *Hermeneutische Wissenssoziologie.* Konstanz, 9–13.

Hörning, K. H. and Winter, R. (Eds.) (1999) *Widerspenstige Kulturen.* Frankfurt/Main.

Howarth, D. (2000) *Discourse.* Buckingham.

Howarth, D. (2009) 'Power, discourse, and policy: articulating a hegemony approach to critical policy studies'. In *Critical Policy Studies* 3 (3–4), 309–335.

Howarth, D. and Torfing, J. (Eds.) (2005) *Discourse Theory in European Politics: Identity, Policy and Governance.* London.

Howarth, D., Norval, A. J. and Stavrakakis, Y. (Eds.) (2000) *Discourse Theory and Political Analysis.* Manchester.

Hutchby, I. and Wooffitt, R. (1988) *Conversation Analysis.* Cambridge.

Jäckle, M. (2008) *Schule M(m)acht Geschlechter. Eine Auseinandersetzung mit Schule und Geschlecht unter diskurstheoretischer Perspektive.* Wiesbaden.

Jacobs, K. (2006) 'Discourse Analysis and its Utility for Urban Policy Research'. In *Urban Policy and Research*, Vol. 24, Nr. 1, 39–52.

Jäger, L. (2010) *Saussure zur Einführung.* Hamburg.

Jäger, M. (2010) 'Die Kritik am Patriarchat im Einwanderungsdiskurs'. In: Keller, R., Hirseland, A., Schneider, W. and Viehöver, W. (Eds.) (2010) *Handbuch Sozialwissenschaftliche Diskursanalyse Vol. 2: Forschungspraxis.* 4. Ed. Wiesbaden [2003], 421–438.

Jäger, M. and Jäger, S. (2007) *Deutungskämpfe. Theorie und Praxis Kritischer Diskursanalyse.* Wiesbaden.

Jäger, S. (1999) 'Einen Königsweg gibt es nicht. Bemerkungen zur Durchführung von Diskursanalysen'. In: Bublitz, H., Bührmann, A. D., Hanke, C. and Seier, A. (Eds.) (1999) *Das Wuchern der Diskurse. Perspektiven der Diskursanalyse Foucaults.* Frankfurt/Main, 136–147.

Jäger, S. (2009) *Kritische Diskursanalyse.* 5. ed. Duisburg [1993].

Jäger, S. (2011) 'Diskurs und Wissen'. In Keller, R., Hirseland, A., Schneider, W. and Viehöver, W. (Eds.) (2011) *Handbuch Sozialwissenschaftliche Diskursanalyse Vol. 1: Theorien und Methoden.* 3. Ed. Wiesbaden [2001], 83–114.

Jäger, S. (Ed.) (1992) *BrandSätze. Rassismus im Alltag.* Duisburg.

Jäger, S. and Zimmermann, J. (Eds.) (2010) *Lexikon der Kritischen Diskursanalyse: Eine Werkzeugkiste.* Münster.

Januschek, F. (Ed.) (1985) *Politische Sprachwissenschaft.* Opladen.

Jaworski, A. and Coupland, N. (Eds.) (2006) *The Discourse Reader.* 2. ed. London.

Jørgensen M. W. and Philipps, L. J. (2002) *Discourse Analysis as Theory and Method.* London.

Jung, M. (2011) 'Diskurshistorische Analyse – eine linguistische Perspektive'. In Keller, R., Hirseland, A., Schneider, W. and Viehöver, W. (Eds.) (2011) *Handbuch*

Sozialwissenschaftliche Diskursanalyse Vol. 1: Theorien und Methoden. 3. Ed. Wiesbaden [2001], 31–54.

Jung, M., Böke, K. and Wengeler, M. (Eds.) (1997) *Die Sprache des Migrationsdiskurses.* Opladen.

Kallmeyer, W. (1985) 'Handlungskonstitution im Gespräch'. In: Gülich, E. and Steger, H. (Eds.) *Grammatik, Konversation, Interaktion.* Tübingen, 81–123.

Kelle, U. and Kluge, S. (1999) *Vom Einzelfall zum Typus.* Opladen.

Keller, R. (1998) *Müll – Die gesellschaftliche Konstruktion des Wertvollen.* Opladen [2. ed. 2009 Wiesbaden].

Keller, R. (2003) *Zum möglichen Verhältnis zwischen Diskursanalyse und Ethnographie.* Unpublished Conference Paper Workshop ,Ethnographie der Arbeit – die Arbeit der Ethnographie'. Berlin.

Keller, R. (2005a) *Wissenssoziologische Diskursanalyse. Grundlegung eines Forschungs-programms.* Wiesbaden [3. Ed. 2011; English translation in preparation for 2013].

Keller, R. (2005b) 'Wissenssoziologische Diskursanalyse als interpretative Analytik'. In: Keller, R., Hirseland, A., Schneider, W. and Viehöver, W. (Eds.) (2005) *Die diskursive Konstruktion von Wirklichkeit.* Konstanz, 49–76.

Keller, R. (2008) *Michel Foucault.* Konstanz.

Keller, R. (2009) 'Das Interpretative Paradigma'. In: Brock, D., Diefenbach, H., Junge, M., Keller, R. and Villanýi, D. (2009) *Soziologische Paradigmen nach Parsons.* Wiesbaden, 17–126.

Keller, R. (2010) 'Der Müll der Gesellschaft'. In Keller, R., Hirseland, A., Schneider, W. and Viehöver, W. (Eds.) (2010) *Handbuch Sozialwissenschaftliche Diskursanalyse Vol. 2: Forschungspraxis.* 4. Ed. Wiesbaden [2003], 197–232.

Keller, R. (2011a) 'Wissenssoziologische Diskursanalyse'. In Keller, R., Hirseland, A., Schneider, W. and Viehöver, W. (Eds.) (2011) *Handbuch Sozialwissenschaftliche Diskursanalyse Vol. 1: Theorien und Methoden.* 3. Ed. Wiesbaden [2001], 115–147.

Keller, R. (2011b). *The Sociology of Knowledge Approach to Discourse (SKAD).* In *Human Studies* 34 (1), 43–65.

Keller, R. (2012): 'Entering Discourses: A New Agenda for Qualitative Research and Sociology of Knowledge'. In *Qualitative Sociology Review* 8 (2), 46–75.

Keller, R. (forthcoming) *The Sociology of Knowledge Approach to Discourse.* New York [translation from Keller 2005a, in preparation].

Keller, R., Hirseland, A., Schneider, W. and Viehöver, W. (Eds.) (2005) *Die diskursive Konstruktion von Wirklichkeit.* Konstanz.

Keller, R., Hirseland, A., Schneider, W. and Viehöver, W. (Eds.) (2011) *Handbuch Sozialwissenschaftliche Diskursanalyse Vol. 1: Theorien und Methoden.* 3. Ed. Wiesbaden [2001].

Keller, R., Hirseland, A., Schneider, W. and Viehöver, W. (Eds.). (2010) *Handbuch Sozial wissenschaftliche Diskursanalyse Vol. 2: Forschungspraxis.* 4. Ed. Wiesbaden [2003].

Keller, R., Schneider, W. and Viehöver, W. (Eds.) (2012) *Diskurs – Macht – Subjekt. Theorie und Praxis der Subjektivierung in der Diskursforschung.* Wiesbaden.

Keller, R. and Truschkat, I. (Eds.) (2012) *Methodologie und Praxis der Wissensso-ziologischen Diskursanalyse Vol. 1* Wiesbaden.

Kellner, D. (1995) *Media Culture.* London.

Kendall, G. and Wickham, G. (1999) *Using Foucault's Methods.* London.

Kerchner, B. and Schneider, S. (Eds.) (2006) *Foucault. Diskursanalyse der Politik: Eine Einführung.* Wiesbaden.

Kluge, S. (1999) *Empirisch begründete Typenbildung.* Opladen.

Knapp, G.-A. and Wetterer, A. (Eds.) (1992) *TraditionenBrüche.* Freiburg.

Knoblauch, H. (1995) *Kommunikationskultur.* Berlin.

Knoblauch, H. (2000) 'Das Ende der linguistischen Wende'. In: *Soziologie* 2, 46–58.

Knoblauch, H. (2001) 'Fokussierte Ethnographie'. In: *Sozialer Sinn* 1, 123–142.

Knoblauch, H. (2005a) 'Focused Ethnography' [30 paragraphs]. In: *Forum Qualitative Sozialforschung / Forum: Qualitative Social Research* 6 (3), Art. 44, http://nbn-resolving. de/urn:nbn:de:0114-fqs0503440 [13.3.2010]

Knoblauch, H. (2005b) *Wissenssoziologie.* Konstanz.

Knoblauch, H. (2011) 'Diskurs, Kommunikation und Wissenssoziologie'. In: Keller, R., Hirseland, A., Schneider, W. and Viehöver,W. (Eds.) (2011) *Handbuch Sozialwissen schaftliche Diskursanalyse Vol. 1: Theorien und Methoden.* 3. Ed. Wiesbaden [2001], 209–226.

Knoblauch, H. and Luckmann, Th. (2004) 'Genre Analysis'. In: Flick, Kardorff and Steinke (Eds.) (2004) *A Companion to Qualitative Research.* London, 303–307.

Knoblauch, H., Baer, A., Laurier, E., Petschke, S. and Schnettler, B. (2008) Visual Analysis. New Developments in the Interpretative Analysis of Video and Photography [30 paragraphs]. In: *Forum Qualitative Sozialforschung / Forum: Qualitative Social Research* 9 (3), Art. 14, http://nbn-resolving.de/urn:nbn:de:0114-fqs0803148 [13.3.2012]

Knoblauch, H., Schnettler, B., Raab, J. and Soeffner, H.-G. (Eds.) (2006) *Video Analysis: Methodology and Methods. Qualitative Audiovisual Data Analysis in Sociology.* Frankfurt/Main.

Knorr-Cetina, K. (1981) *The Manufacture of Knowledge – An Essay on the Constructivist and Contextual Nature of Science.* Oxford.

Kohlhaas, P. (2000) 'Diskurs und Modell'. In: Nennen, H.-U. (Ed.) (2000) *Diskurs. Begriff und Realisierung.* Würzburg, 29–56.

Konerding, K. (2009) 'Diskurslinguistik – eine neue linguistische Teildisziplin'. In: Felder, E. (Ed.) (2009) *Sprache.* Heidelberg, 155–178.

Korte, H. and Drexler P. (2000) *Einführung in die systematische Filmanalyse.* Berlin.

Krais, B. (1993) 'Geschlechterverhältnis und symbolische Gewalt'. In: Gebauer, G. and Wulf, G. (Eds.) *Praxis und Ästhetik.* Frankfurt/Main, 208–250.

Kress, G. and van Leeuwen, T. (2001) *Multimodal Discourse. The Modes and Media of Contemporary Communication.* London.

DOING DISCOURSE RESEARCH

Kress, G. and van Leeuwen, T. (2006) *Reading Images*. London.

Lacan, J. (2007) *Ecrits. The First Complete Edition in English*. New York/London.

Laclau, E. (1977) *Politics and Ideology in Marxist Theory*. London.

Laclau, E. (1990) *New Reflections on the Revolutions of Our Time*. London.

Laclau, E. (1993) 'Discourse'. In: Goodin, R. and Pettit, Ph. (Eds.) *A Companion to Contemporary Political Philosophy*. Oxford, 431–437.

Laclau, E. (1994) 'Why do Empty Signifiers Matter to Politics?' In: Weeks, J. (Ed.) *The Lesser Evil and the Greater Good*. London, 167–178.

Laclau, E. (1996) *Emancipation(s)*. London.

Laclau, E. and Mouffe, G. (1985) *Hegemony and Socialist Strategy*. London/New York

Landwehr, A. (2001) *Geschichte des Sagbaren. Einführung in die Historische Diskursanalyse*. Tübingen.

Landwehr, A. (2008) *Historische Diskursanalyse*. Frankfurt/Main.

Landwehr, A. (Ed.) (2010) *Diskursiver Wandel*. Wiesbaden.

Langer, A. (2008) *Disziplinieren und entspannen: Körper in der Schule – eine diskursanalytische Ethnographie*. Bielefeld.

Latour, B. (1987) *Science in Action*. Cambridge.

Latour, B. (1993) *We Have Never Been Modern*. Harvard.

Latour, B. and Woolgar, S. (1988) *La vie de laboratoire*. Paris [English original version: *Laboratory Life*, Beverly Hills 1979].

Leeuwen, T. van and Jewitt, C. (Eds.) (2001) *Handbook of Visual Analysis*. London.

Leeuwen, T. van (2005) *Introducing Social Semiotics*. London

Leeuwen, T. van (2008) *Discourse and Practice. New Tools for Critical Discourse Analysis*. Oxford.

Leontiev, A. N. (1978). *Activity, Consciousness and Personality*. New York.

Link, J. (1982) 'Kollektivsymbolik und Mediendiskurse'. In: *kultuRRevolution* 1, 6–21.

Link, J. (1983) *Elementare Literatur und generative Diskursanalyse*. München.

Link, J. (1984) 'Über ein Modell synchroner Systeme von Kollektivsymbolen sowie seine Rolle bei der Diskurskonstitution'. In: Link, J. and Wülfing, W. (Eds.) (1984) *Bewegung und Stillstand in Metaphern und Mythen*. Stuttgart, 63–92.

Link, J. (1988) 'Über Kollektivsymbolik im politischen Diskurs und ihren Anteil an totalitären Tendenzen'. In: *kultuRRevolution* 17/18, 47–53.

Link, J. (1995) 'Diskurstheorie'. In: Haug, W.-F. (Ed.) *Historisch-kritisches Wörterbuch des Marxismus*, Vol. 2. Hamburg, 744–748.

Link, J. (1997) *Versuch über den Normalismus*. Opladen.

Link, J. (1999) 'Diskursive Ereignisse, Diskurse, Interdiskurse'. In: Bublitz, H., Bührmann, A. D., Hanke, C. and Seier, A. (Eds.) (1999) *Das Wuchern der Diskurse. Perspektiven der Diskursanalyse Foucaults*. Frankfurt/Main 148–161.

Link, J. (2011) 'Diskursanalyse unter besonderer Berücksichtigung von Interdiskurs und Kollektivsymbolik'. In: Keller, R., Hirseland, A., Schneider, W. and Viehöver, W.

(Eds.) (2011) *Handbuch Sozialwissenschaftliche Diskursanalyse Vol. 1: Theorien und Methoden.* 3. Ed. Wiesbaden [2001], 407–430.

Link, J. and Link-Heer, U. (1990) 'Diskurs/Interdiskurs und Literaturanalyse'. In: *Zeitschrift für Linguistik und Literaturwissenschaft* (LiLi) 77, 88–99.

Litfin, K. (1994) *Ozone Discourse.* New York.

Luckmann, T. (1979) 'Soziologie der Sprache'. In: König, R. (Ed.) *Handbuch der empirischen Sozialforschung,* Vol. 13. Stuttgart, 1–116.

Luckmann, T. (1999) 'Wirklichkeiten: individuelle Konstitution und gesellschaftliche Konstruktion'. In: Hitzler, R., Reichertz, J. and Schröer, N. (Eds.) (1999) *Hermeneutische Wissenssoziologie. Standpunkte zur Theorie der Interpretation.* Konstanz, 17–28.

Lüders, C. (2004) 'Fieldwork Observation and Ethnography'. In: Flick, Kardorff and Steinkel. (Eds.) (2004) *A Companion to Qualitative Research.* London, 222–230.

Lüders, C. and Meuser, M. (1997) 'Deutungsmusteranalyse'. In: Hitzler, R. and Honer, A. (Eds.) (1997) *Sozialwissenschaftliche Hermeneutik.* Opladen, 57–80.

Maas, U. (1988) 'Probleme und Traditionen der Diskursanalyse'. In: *Zeitschrift für Phonetik, Sprachwissenschaft und Kommunikationsforschung* 41, 717–729.

Maas, U. (1989) *Sprachpolitik und politische Sprachwissenschaft.* Frankfurt/Main.

Maasen, S. (1998) *Genealogie der Unmoral.* Frankfurt/Main.

Maasen, S. (2010) 'Zur Therapeutisierung sexueller Selbste'. In: Keller, R., Hirseland, A., Schneider, W. and Viehöver, W. (Eds.) (2010) *Handbuch Sozialwissenschaftliche Diskursanalyse Vol. 2: Forschungspraxis.* 4. Ed. Wiesbaden [2003], 119–146.

Maasen, S., Mayerhauser, T. and Renggli, C. (Eds.) (2006) *Bilder als Diskurse – Bilddiskurse.* Weilerswist.

Macdonell, D. (1986) *Theories of Discourse. An Introduction.* Oxford.

Maihofer, A. (1995) *Geschlecht als Existenzweise.* Frankfurt/Main.

Maingueneau, D. (1976) *Initiation aux méthodes de l'analyse du discours.* Paris.

Maingueneau, D. (1991) *L'Analyse du discours.* Paris.

Maingueneau, D. (1994) 'Die ,französische Schule' der Diskursanalyse'. In: Ehlich, K. (Ed.) (1994) *Diskursanalyse in Europa.* Frankfurt/Main, 187–195.

Maingueneau, D. (Ed.) (1995) 'Les analyses du discours en France'. *Langages* 117 [special issue].

Maingueneau, D. (2012) 'Äußerungsszene und Subjektivität'. In: Keller, R. Schneider, W. and Viehöver, W. (Eds.) (2012) *Diskurs - Macht - Subjekt.* Wiesbaden, 165–190.

Manghani, S., Piper, A. and Simon, J. (Eds.) (2006) *Images: A Reader.* London.

Marotzki, W. and Niesyto, H. (Eds.) (2006) *Bildinterpretation und Bildverstehen: Methodische Ansätze aus sozialwissenschaftlicher, kunst- und medienpädagogischer Perspektive.* Wiesbaden.

Martschukat, J. (2000) *Inszeniertes Töten.* Köln.

Marxhausen, Ch. (2010) *Identität – Repräsentation – Diskurs. Eine handlungsorientierte linguistische Diskursanalyse zur Erfassung raumbezogener Identitätsangebote.* Stuttgart.

McCarthy, E. D. (1996) *Knowledge as Culture.* London.

McHoul, A. (1994) 'Discourse'. In: Asher, R. E. and Simpson, J. M. Y. (Eds.) *The Encyclopedia of Language and Linguistics,* Vol. 2. Oxford, 940–949.

McNay, L. (1992) *Foucault and Feminism.* Boston.

Mead, G. H. (1934) *Mind, Self, and Society.* Ed. by C. W. Morris. Chicago.

Meier, S. (2008) *(Bild-)Diskurs im Netz: Konzept und Methode für eine semiotische Diskursanalyse im Word Wide Web.* Köln.

Meier, S. (2011) 'Multimodalität im Diskurs. Konzept und Methoden einer multi- modalen Diskursanalyse'. In: Keller, R., Hirseland, A., Schneider, W. and Viehöver, W. (Eds.) (2011) *Handbuch Sozialwissenschaftliche Diskursanalyse Vol. 1: Theorien und Methoden.* 3. Ed. Wiesbaden [2001] 499–532.

Meuser, M. and Sackmann, R. (Eds.) (1992) *Analysen sozialer Deutungsmuster.* Pfaffenweiler.

Mikos, L. (2008) *Film- und Fernsehanalyse.* 2nd revised edition. Konstanz.

Mikos, L. and Wegener, C. (Eds.) (2005) *Qualitative Medienforschung. Ein Handbuch.* Konstanz.

Miller, G. and Fox, K. J. (2004) 'Building Bridges: The Possibility of Analytic Dialogue Between Ethnography, Conversation Analysis and Foucault'. In: Silverman, D. (Ed.) *Qualitative Research.* London, 35–55.

Mills, S. (2004) *Discourse.* London/New York.

Modan, G. G. (2007) *Turf Wars. Discourse, Diversity and the Politics of Place.* Oxford.

Mottier, V. (2002) 'Discourse Analysis and the Politics of Identity/Difference'. In: *European Political Science* Vol. 2, Nr. 1 [Online-Journal: www.essex.ac.uk/ecpr/ publications/eps/onlineisssues/autumn2002; 29.7.2003]

Müller-Doohm, S. (1996) 'Die kulturelle Kodierung des Schlafens oder: Wovon das Schlafzimmer ein Zeichen ist'. In: *Soziale Welt* 47 (1), 110–122.

Naples, N. (2003) *Feminism and Method: Ethnography, Discourse Analysis, and Activist Research.* London.

Nennen, H.-U. (Ed.) (2000) *Diskurs. Begriff und Realisierung.* Würzburg.

Nennen, H.-U. (2000a) 'Zur Einführung'. In: Nennen, H.-U. (Ed.) (2000) *Diskurs. Begriff und Realisierung.* Würzburg, VII–XXV.

Niehr, T. and Böke, K. (Eds.) (2000) *Einwanderungsdiskurse.* Opladen.

Niehr T. and Böke, K. (2010) 'Diskursanalyse unter linguistischer Perspektive'. In: Keller, R., Hirseland, A., Schneider, W. and Viehöver, W. (Eds.) (2010) *Handbuch Sozialwissenschaftliche Diskursanalyse Bd. 2: Forschungspraxis.* 4. Ed. Wiesbaden [2003], 325–352.

Nonhoff, M. (2006) *Politischer Diskurs und Hegemonie. Das Projekt Soziale Marktwirtschaft.* Bielefeld.

Nonhoff, M. (Ed.) (2007) *Diskurs – radikale Demokratie – Hegemonie.* Bielefeld.

Nowotny, H. (1999) *Es ist so. Es könnte auch anders sein.* Frankfurt/Main.

Omi, M. and Winant, H. (1994). *Racial Formations in the United States*. New York:

Paltridge, B. (2007) *Discourse Analysis. An Introduction*. London.

Parker, I. (1992) *Discourse dynamics*. London.

Parker, I. and The Bolton Discourse Network (Eds.) (1999) *Critical Textwork: An Introduction to Varieties of Discourse and Analysis*. Buckingham.

Parr, R. and Thiele, M. (2010) *Link(s). Eine Bibliographie zu den Konzepten ›Interdiskurs‹, ›Kollektivsymbolik‹ und ›Normalismus‹ sowie einigen weiteren Fluchtlinien*. 2. Ed. Heidelberg.

Pêcheux, M. (1984) 'Metapher und Interdiskurs'. In: Link, J. and Wülfing, W. (Eds.) (1984) *Bewegung und Stillstand in Metaphern und Mythen*. Stuttgart, 93–99.

Pêcheux, M. (1988) 'Sind die Massen ein beseeltes Objekt?' In: *kultuRRevolution* 17/18, 7–12.

Pêcheux, M. (1995) *Automatic Discourse Analysis*. Utrecht [1969].

Perrow, Ch. (1999) *Normal Accidents*. Princeton.

Philipps, N. and Hardy, C. (2002) *Discourse Analysis*. London.

Pickering, A. (1995) *The Mangle of Practice. Time, Agency, and Science*. Chicago.

Plaß, C. and Schetsche, M. (2001) 'Grundzüge einer wissenssoziologischen Theorie sozialer Deutungsmuster'. In: *Sozialer Sinn* 1, 511–536.

Plummer, K. (Ed.) (1991) *Symbolic Interactionism*. 2 Vol. Aldershot.

Pocock, J. G. A. (1962) 'The history of political thought'. In: Laslett, P. and Runciman, W.G. (Eds.) *Philosophy, Politics and Society*. Oxford, 183–202.

Pocock, J. G. A. (1965) *The Machiavellian Moment*. Princeton.

Poferl, A. (1997) 'Der strukturkonservative Risikodiskurs'. In: Brand, K.-W., Eder, K. and Poferl, A. (Eds.) (1997) *Ökologische Kommunikation in Deutschland*. Opladen, 106–154.

Poferl, A. (2004) *Die Kosmopolitik des Alltags*. Berlin.

Potter, J. (1996) *Representing Reality*. London.

Potter, J. (Ed.) (2007) *Discourse and Psychology*. London.

Potter, J. and Wetherell, M. (1987) *Discourse and Social Psychology*. London.

Potter, J. and Wetherell, M. (1998) 'Social representations, discourse analysis, and racism'. In: Flick, U. (Ed.) *The Psychology of the Social*. Cambridge, 138—155.

Power, R. (2000) *A Question of Knowledge*. Harlow.

Prittwitz, Volker v. (Ed.) (1996) *Verhandeln und Argumentieren. Dialog, Interessen und Macht in der Umweltpolitik*. Opladen.

Psathas, G. (1995) *Conversation Analysis*. Thousand Oaks.

Raab, H. (1998) *Foucault und der feministische Poststrukturalismus*. Dortmund.

Raab, J. (2008) *Visuelle Wissenssoziologie*. Konstanz.

Reckwitz, A. (2000) *Die Transformation der Kulturtheorien*. Weilerswist.

Reichertz, J. (1997) 'Objektive Hermeneutik'. In: Hitzler, R. and Honer, A. (Eds.) *Sozialwissenschaftliche Hermeneutik*. Opladen, 31–55.

Reichertz, J. (2009) 'Abduction: The Logic of Discovery of Grounded Theory' [39 paragraphs]. In: Forum Qualitative Sozialforschung / Forum: Qualitative Social Research, 11(1), Art. 13, http://nbn-resolving.de/urn:nbn:de:0114-fqs1001135 [15.3.2011]

Reichertz, J. and Schröer, N. (1994) 'Erheben, Auswerten, Darstellen'. In: Schröer, N. (Ed.) (1994) Interpretative Sozialforschung. Opladen, 56–84.

Ricken, N. (2006) Die Ordnung der Bildung. Wiesbaden.

Ricoeur, P. (1974) The Conflict of Interpretations. Evanston.

Ricoeur, P. (1977) 'Diskurs und Kommunikation'. In: Neue Hefte für Philosophie, Vol. 11, 1–25.

Ricoeur, P. (1981) 'The Model of the Text: Meaningful Action Considered as a Text'. In Ricoeur, P. (1981): Hermeneutics and the Human Sciences. Cambridge, 197–221.

Ricoeur, P. (1990) Time and Narrative. 3 Volumes. Chicago [1983].

Rogers, R. (Ed.) (2011) An Introduction to Critical Discourse Research in Education. 2. ed. London.

Rorty, R. (Ed.) (1967) The Linguistic Turn. Chicago.

Rorty, R. (1979) Philosophy and the Mirror of Nature. Princeton.

Rorty, R. (1989) Contingency, Irony, and Solidarity. Cambridge.

Rose, G. (2001) Visual Methodologies. London.

Rose, G. (2007) Visual Methodologies. An Introduction to the Interpretation of Visual Materials. 2. Ed. London.

Rose, N., O'Malley, P. and Valverde, M. (2009) 'Governmentality'. In: Annual Review of Law and Social Science, Vol. 2, 83–104.

Sachs-Hombach, K. and Rehkämper, K. (Eds.) (2000) Bild – Bildwahrnehmung – Bildverarbeitung. Opladen.

Said, E. (1979) Orientalism. New York.

Sarasin, P. (1996) 'Subjekte, Diskurse, Körper'. In: Hardtwig, W. and Wehler, H.-U. (Eds.) Kulturgeschichte Heute (Geschichte und Gesellschaft, Special Issue 16), 131–164.

Sarasin, P. (2001) Reizbare Maschinen. Eine Geschichte des Körpers 1765–1914. Frankfurt/Main.

Sarasin, P. (2003) Geschichtswissenschaft und Diskursanalyse. Frankfurt/Main

Sarasin, P. (2011) 'Diskurstheorie und Geschichtswissenschaft'. In: Keller, R., Hirseland, A., Schneider, W. and Viehöver, W. (Eds.) (2011) Handbuch Sozialwissenschaftliche Diskursanalyse Vol. 1: Theorien und Methoden. 3. Ed. Wiesbaden [2001], 55–82.

Saussure, F. de (1965) Course In General Linguistics. Oxford [1916].

Saville-Troike, M. (2003) The Ethnography of Communication. Oxford.

Schalk, H. (1997/98) 'Diskurs'. In: Archiv für Begriffsgeschichte 40, 56–104.

Schetsche, M. (1996) Die Karriere sozialer Probleme. München.

Schiebinger, L. (2004) Nature's Body: Gender in the Making of Modern Science. New Brunswick.

Schiffrin, D. (1994) *Approaches to Discourse*. Oxford.

Schiffrin, D., Tannen, D. and Hamilton, H. E. (Eds.) (2001) *The Handbook of Discourse Analysis*. Malden.

Schmidt, V. (2009) 'Taking Ideas And Discourse Seriously: Explaining Change Through Discursive Institutionalism as the Fourth "New Institutionalism". In: *European Political Science Review* 2 (1), 1–25.

Schmied-Knittel, I. (2008) *Satanismus und ritueller Missbrauch. Eine wissenssoziologische Diskursanalyse*. Würzburg.

Schneider, J. G. (Ed.) (2008) Medialität und Sozialität sprachlicher Zeichen. *Zeitschrift für Semiotik* 30 (1–2) [Special Issue].

Schneider, W. (1999) *'So tot wie nötig – so lebendig wie möglich!' Sterben und Tod in der fortgeschrittenen Moderne*. Münster.

Schröer, N. (Ed.) (1994) *Interpretative Sozialforschung*. Opladen.

Schröer, N. (1997) 'Wissenssoziologische Hermeneutik'. In: Hitzler, R. and Honer, A. (Eds.) *Sozialwissenschaftliche Hermeneutik*. Opladen, 109–132.

Schütz, Alfred (1967) *The Phenomenology of the Social World*. Evanston [1932].

Schütze, Y. (1992) 'Das Deutungsmuster "Mutterliebe" im historischen Wandel'. In: Meuser, M. and Sackmann, R. (Eds.) (1992) *Analysen sozialer Deutungsmuster*. Pfaffenweiler, 39–48.

Schwab-Trapp M. (2010) 'Methodische Aspekte der Diskursanalyse'. In: Keller, R., Hirseland, A., Schneider, W. and Viehöver, W. (Eds.) (2010) *Handbuch Sozialwissenschaftliche Diskursanalyse Vol. 2: Forschungspraxis*. 4. Ed. Wiesbaden [2003], 169–196.

Schwab-Trapp, M. (2011) 'Diskurs als soziologisches Konzept'. In: Keller, R., Hirseland, A., Schneider, W. and Viehöver, W. (Eds.) (2011) *Handbuch Sozialwissenschaftliche Diskursanalyse Vol. 1: Theorien und Methoden*. 3. Ed. Wiesbaden [2001], 263–286.

Singelnstein, T. (2009) *Diskurs und Kriminalität: Außergesetzliche Anwendungsregeln als diskursive Praktiken im Wechselverhältnis zwischen Kriminalisierungsdiskursen und Strafrechtsanwendung*. Berlin.

Skinner, Q. (1978) *The Foundations of Modern Political Thought, 2 Vol*. Cambridge

Smart, Barry (2002) *Michel Foucault*. 2. Ed. London.

Smith, M. (2008) *Visual Culture Studies. Interviews with Key Thinkers*. London.

Soeffner, H.-G. (1989) *Auslegung des Alltags – Der Alltag der Auslegung*. Frankfurt/Main.

Soeffner, H.-G. (2004) *'Social Scientific Hermeneutics'*. In: Flick, Kardorff and Steinke (Eds.) (2004) *A Companion to Qualitative Research*. London, 95–100.

Soeffner, H.-G. (Ed.) (1979) *Interpretative Verfahren in den Sozial- und Textwissenschaften*. Stuttgart.

Soeffner, H.-G. and Hitzler, R. (1994) 'Hermeneutik als Haltung und Handlung'. In: Schröer, N. (Ed.) *Interpretative Sozialforschung*. Opladen, 28–55.

Spivak, G. C. (1990) *The Post-Colonial Critic*. New York.

Sprondel, W. (Ed.) (1994) *Die Objektivität der Ordnungen und ihre kommunikative Konstruktion*. Frankfurt/Main.

Stäheli, U. (1999) 'Die politische Theorie der Hegemonie: Ernesto Laclau und Chantal Mouffe'. In: Brodocz, A. and Schaal, G. (Eds.) (1999) *Politische Theorien der Gegenwart*. Opladen, 143–166.

Stäheli, U. (2000) *Poststrukturalistische Soziologien*. Bielefeld.

Steinmetz, W. (1993) *Das Sagbare und das Machbare. Zum Wandel politischer Handlungsspielräume; England 1780–1867*. Stuttgart.

Stöckl, H. (2004) *Die Sprache im Bild – Das Bild in der Sprache*. Berlin.

Strauss, A. (1987) *Qualitative Research for Social Scientists*. Cambridge.

Strauss, A. (1991) *Creating Sociological Awareness*. New Brunswick.

Strauss, A. (1998) *Grundlagen qualitativer Sozialforschung*. München [German Translation of Strauss 1987].

Strauss, A. and Corbin, J. (1998) *Basics of Qualitative Research*. 2. Ed. London.

Strauss, C. and Quinn, N. (1997) *A Cognitive Theory of Cultural Meaning*. Cambridge.

Sturken, M. and Cartwright, L. (2005) *Practices of Looking. An Introduction to Visual Culture*. New York. [2001].

Ten Have, P. (2007) *Doing Conversation Analysis. A Practical Guide*. 2. Ed. London.

Teubert, W. (1999) 'Korpuslinguistik und Lexikographie'. In: *Deutsche Sprache* 27 (4), 292–313.

Teubert, W. (2010a) *Meaning, Discourse and Society*. Cambridge.

Teubert, W. (2010b) 'Rethinking corpus linguistics'. In: Sánchez, A. and Almela, M. (Eds.) *A Mosaic of Corpus Linguistics*. Frankfurt/Main, 19–42.

Titscher, S., Wodak, R., Meyer, M. and Vetter, E. (2000) *Methods of Text and Discourse Analysis*. London.

Toolan, M. J. (Ed.) (2002) *Critical Discourse Analysis*. London.

Torfing, J. (1999) *New Theories of Discourse. Laclau, Mouffe and Žižek*. Oxford.

Truschkat, I. (2008) *Kompetenzdiskurs und Bewerbungsgespräche: Eine Dispositivanalyse (neuer) Rationalitäten sozialer Differenzierung*. Wiesbaden.

Tully, J. (Ed.) (1988a) *Meaning and Context*. Cambridge.

Tully, J. (1988b) 'The pen is a mighty sword: Quentin Skinner's analysis of politics'. In: Tully, J. (Ed.) (1988a) *Meaning and Context*. Cambridge, 7–28.

Ullrich, P. (2008) *Die Linke, Israel und Palästina. Nahostdiskurse in Großbritannien und Deutschland*. Berlin.

Viehöver, W. (2010) 'Governing the Planetary Greenhouse in Spite of Scientific Uncertainty'. In: *Science, Technology and Innovation Studies*, Vol. 6, No 2, 127–154.

Viehöver, W. (2011) 'Diskurse als Narrationen'. In: Keller, R., Hirseland, A., Schneider, W. and Viehöver, W. (Eds.) (2011) *Handbuch Sozialwissenschaftliche Diskursanalyse Vol. 1: Theorien und Methoden*. 3. Ed. Wiesbaden [2001], 179–208.

Viehöver, W., Keller, R. and Schneider, W. (Eds.) (2012) *Wissen, Sprache, Diskurs.* Wiesbaden.

Völter, B., Dausien, B., Lutz, H. and Rosenthal, G. (Eds.) (2009) *Biographieforschung im Diskurs.* 2. Ed. Wiesbaden.

Waldschmidt, A. (1996) *Das Subjekt in der Humangenetik.* Münster.

Waldschmidt, A. (2010) 'Der Humangenetik-Diskurs der Experten'. In: Keller, R., Hirseland, A., Schneider, W. and Viehöver, W. (Eds.) (2010) *Handbuch Sozialwissen schaftliche Diskursanalyse Vol. 2: Forschungspraxis.* 4. Ed. Wiesbaden [2003], 147–168.

Waldschmidt, A., Klein, A. and Korte, M. T. (2009) *Das Wissen der Leute. Bioethik, Alltag und Macht im Internet.* Wiesbaden.

Warnke, I. (Ed.) (2007) *Diskurslinguistik nach Foucault. Theorie und Gegenstände.* Berlin.

Warnke, I. and Spitzmüller, J. (Eds.) (2008) *Methoden der Diskurslinguistik. Sprachwissenschaftliche Zugänge zur transtextuellen Ebene.* Berlin.

Warnke, I. and Spitzmüller, J. (2008a) 'Methoden und Methodologie der Diskurslinguistik. Grundlagen und Verfahren einer Sprachwissenschaft jenseits textueller Grenzen'. In: Warnke, I. and Spitzmüller, J. (Eds.) (2008) *Methoden der Diskurslinguistik. Sprachwissenschaftliche Zugänge zur transtextuellen Ebene.* Berlin, 3–54.

Warnke, I. and Spitzmüller, J. (2011) 'Discourse as a "linguistic object". Methodical and methodological delimitations'. In *Critical Discourse Studies* 8, 2, 75–94.

Weiss, G. and Wodak, R. (Eds.) (2003) *Critical Discourse Analysis.* London.

Wengeler, M. (2003) *Topos und Diskurs.* Tübingen.

Wetherell, M. (1998) 'Positioning and interpretative repertoires: conversation analysis and post-structuralism in dialogue'. In *Discourse and Society* 9 (3), 387–412.

Wetherell, M., Taylor, S. and Yates, S. J. (Eds.) (2001a) *Discourse Theory and Practice.* London.

Wetherell, M., Taylor, S. and Yates, S. J. (Eds.) (2001b) *Discourse as Data.* London.

White, H. (1975) *Metahistory: The Historical Imagination in Nineteenth-Century Europe.* Baltimore.

Widdowson, H.G. (2004) *Text, Context, Pretext. Critical Issues in Discourse Analysis.* Oxford.

Widdowson, H.G. (2007) *Discourse Analysis.* Oxford.

Williams, G. (1999) *French Discourse Analysis.* London.

Winter, R. (1999) 'Cultural Studies als kritische Medienanalyse'. In: Hepp, A. and Winter, R. (Eds.) (1999) *Kultur – Macht – Medien.* Opladen, 49–66.

Winter, R. and Mikos, L. (2001) *Die Fabrikation des Populären.* Bielefeld.

Wittgenstein, L. (1984) *Werkausgabe Vol 1: Tractatus logico-philosophicus, Tagebücher 1914 – 1916, Philosophische Untersuchungen.* Frankfurt/Main [English translation: Tractatus Logico-Philosophicus, London 1994].

Wobbe, T. and Lindemann, G. (Eds.) (1994) *Denkachsen.* Frankfurt/Main.

Wodak, R. (1986) *Language Behavior in Therapy Groups.* Los Angeles.

Wodak, R. (1996) *Disorders of Discourse*. London.

Wodak, R. (1997) *Gender and Discourse*. London.

Wodak, R. and Chilton, P. (Eds.) (2005) *A New Agenda in (Critical) Discourse Analysis. Theory, Methodology and Interdisciplinarity*. Amsterdam.

Wodak, R. and Krzyzanowski, M. (Eds.) (2008) *Qualitative Discourse Analysis in the Social Sciences*. Hampshire.

Wodak, R. and Ludwig, C. (Eds.) (1999) *Challenges in a Changing World*. Wien.

Wodak, R. and Meyer, M. (Eds.) (2002) *Methods of Critical Discourse Analysis*. London [2. Aufl. 2009].

Wodak, R., Nowak, P., Pelikan, J., Gruber, H., de Cillia, R. and Mitten, R. (1990) *Wir sind alle unschuldige Täter!* Frankfurt/Main.

Wodak, R., de Cillia, R. and Reisigl, M. (1998) *Zur diskursiven Konstruktion nationaler Identität*. Frankfurt/Main.

Wood, L. A. and Kroger, R. O. (2000) *Doing Discourse Analysis*. Thousand Oaks.

Wrana, D. (2006) *Das Subjekt schreiben. Subjektivierung und reflexive Praktiken in der Weiterbildung – Eine Diskursanalyse*. Baltmannsweiler.

Wundrak, R. (2010) *Die chinesische Community in Bukarest: Eine rekonstruktive, diskursanalytische Fallstudie über Immigration und Transnationalismus*. Wiesbaden.

Wuthnow, R. (1989) *Communities of Discourse*. Cambridge.

Ziem, A. (2008) *Frames und sprachliches Wissen. Kognitive Aspekte der semantischen Kompetenz*. Berlin.

Zimmermann, Ch. (2009) *Familie als Konfliktfeld im amerikanischen Kulturkampf: Eine Diskursanalyse*. Wiesbaden.

Index

27–8; ways of using textual data in 95; *see also* 'archaeological' discourse analysis; culturalist discourse analysis; 'genealogical' discourse analysis
'discourse ethics' (Habermas), 2, 10–11
discourse ethnography, 102–3
discourse linguistics, 17–18, 22
discourse research, 2, 12, 112, 129, 135–6; audio-visual and other non-textual media in, 87, 94, 101, 103–5; conceptual stages in, 92; difference between *linguistic* and *social science* types, 74–6, 112; as distinct from discourse analysis, 2, 101; expansion of, 1, 4; getting started on, 89–92; as interpretative work, 82–4; process of, 69–87; terminology of, 72–4; *see also* empirical discourse research
'discourse studies' (Van Dijk), 15
discourse theories, 3–4, 16, 42–60
'discursive field' (Wuthnow), 42
discursive psychology, 12, 14–16
dispositifs, 52–3, 71–4, 78–9, 84, 87, 102–3
distribution linguistics, 20
Donati, P.R., 38
Dosse, F., 9
Dreyfus, H., 82, 107
Duden, B., 60
Durkheim, E., 7, 63

educational studies, 65
empirical discourse research, 65, 67, 69, 81, 132
'empty signifiers' (Laclau), 57
epistemological structures, 9
ethnography, 102–3
everyday meaning of 'discourse', 5–6
everyday representations, discourses manifested in, 80
exploratory interviews, 93

Fairclough, N., 22–3, 25–7
feminist theory, 59–60
Ferree, M.M., 96
Fiske, J., 58
Flick, U., 90
'formal structure' of an utterance, 111
'formation rules' (Foucault), 46–8
Foucault, M., 2, 8–12, 17–24, 29, 42–3, 46–67, 72, 76, 79, 82, 104, 107
frame analysis, 37
Freitag, W., 66

French school of discourse analysis, 19–20
functional pragmatics, 15

Gamson, W.A., 33, 37–9, 132
Gee, J.P., 12, 14, 108
gender relations, 60
'genealogical' discourse analysis, 50–4
Gerhards, J., 11
Giddens, A., 3–4, 63–4, 72, 79
Glasze, G., 66
Goffman, E., 37, 103
Gottweis, H., 44, 96
Graefen, G., 15
Gramsci, A., 23–4, 55
grounded theory, 66, 97, 100, 109, 114, 117–18, 122
Guilhaumou, J., 82, 132
Gusfield, J.R., 33, 39–41

Habermas, J., 2, 11, 65
habitus concept, 33–4
Hajer, M., 44, 95
Hall, S., 58
Hardy, C., 12, 14
Hark, S., 60
Harris, Z., 6, 20
'hegemonial discourses', 57
'hegemony' concept (Gramsci), 23–4
hermeneutic sociology of knowledge, 62, 112
hermeneutic textual interpretation, 82–3
'historians' dispute' (*Historikerstreit*), 19
Hitzler, R., 80, 83
Honer, A., 83
Howarth, D., 12, 55–6

'ideologies', concept of (Althusser), 23–4
interpretation of overall results from research, 133
interpretative analytics, 81–2, 112–27
interpretative policy analysis, 65
interpretative repertoires, 131

Jäger, S., 22–3, 28–32
Jaworski, A., 12, 14
Jørgensen, M.W., 12, 56
Jung, M., 21

Kallmeyer, W., 16
Keller, R. (author), 12, 62–70, 95–6, 107–8, 123, 125

Kendall, G., 48–9
Knoblauch, H., 102–3, 108
Knorr-Cetina, K., 102
knowledge *see* hermeneutic sociology of
    knowledge; orders of knowledge;
    sociology of knowledge approach
    to discourse
knowledge society, 4
Konerding, K., 17
Koselleck, R., 20
Krais, B., 34
Kristeva, J., 9
Kritische Diskursanalyse, 22–3, 28–32;
    procedure of, 31
Krzyzanowski, M., 12–13

Lacan, J., 10, 55, 57
Laclau, E., 42, 55–9, 66–7, 80
Landwehr, A., 12, 17, 108–9
language games, 4
langue, 7–10
Latour, B., 102
Leeuwen, T. van, 23
Leontiev, A.N., 29–30
Lévi-Strauss, C., 7–8
linguistic discourse history, 20–1
linguistic-rhetorical structure of an
    utterance, 111
linguistics *see* corpus linguistics;
    discourse linguistics
Link, J., 29–31, 79
Link-Heer, U., 29
literature review process, 92–3
Litfin, K., 96
logic of difference and *logic of
    equivalence*, 56
Luckmann, T., 61, 63

Maasen, S., 44, 96
MacDonell, D., 12
macrostructure and *microstructure* of text,
    108–9
Maingueneau, D., 18, 49–50
Martschukat, J., 44
Marx, K., 63
Mattissek, A., 66
Mead, G.H., 6
meaning patterns, 121–4, 132
memos, 109, 119, 121
Modan, G.G., 66
Modigliani, A., 39
Mouffe, C., 42, 55, 58–9, 66–7, 80

multi-methodological nature of discourse, 81
multimodality, 18

narrative analysis, 125–6
narrative structure, 124–7
'natural' data, 86, 94, 110–11
Nietzsche, F., 9, 52
Nonhoff, M., 56
Nowotny, H., 4

orders of knowledge, 2–3, 9, 53, 75, 81,
    84, 89

Paltridge, B., 12
Panofsky, E., 105
Parker, I., 14, 102–3
parole, 8–9
Pêcheux, M., 12, 20, 28
Peirce, C.S., 6
Perrow, C., 124
phenomenal structure, 114–21, 126
Philipps, L.J., 12
Philipps, N., 12, 14
Phillips, L., 56
Pocock, J., 17
post-colonialism, 58–9
post-structuralism, 7, 10
Potter, J., 15–16, 131
'practice' concept in research, 70–1
public discourse, 73, 76–9, 90

qualitative data analysis, software
    programs for, 114
qualitative research, 67, 84, 91, 107, 133

Rabinow, P., 82, 107
reception aesthetics, 10
Reckwitz, A., 54
reflexivity of discourse research, 69;
    see also self-reflective stance
Ricoeur, P., 9, 82

Said, E.W., 59
Sarasin, P., 44, 51, 96
Saussure, F. de, 6–8
Schegloff, E.A., 23
Schmidt, V., 65
Schneider, W., 13, 95, 114
Schütz, A., 63, 126
self-reflective stance, 84
semiotics, 59
Skinner, Q., 17, 20

social practices, data on, 94
social semiotics, 104
sociology of knowledge approach to
    discourse (SKAD), 61–70, 74, 77, 84
Spitzmüller, J., 22
Spivak, G.C., 59
Stäheli, U., 57–8
storylines, 124–5
Strauss, A., 114
structuralism, 6–10
structurization theory (Giddens), 79
subject positions in discourse research,
    74, 79

text-centred nature of discourse
    research, 101, 133
texts for study, selection of, 97
theoretical sampling, 97, 100–1, 130
Titscher, S., 25
Torfing, J., 55–6
translation in actor-network theory, 102
triangulation, 87, 101, 113
truth, regimes of, 52

Urban Studies (journal), 66
utterance: definition of, 72, 74;
    structure of, 111

validity of research, 86–7
Viehöver, W., 96, 108, 125–6
'visual methodologies' in discourse
    analysis, 105

Waldschmidt, A., 44, 80, 96
Warburg, A., 105
Warnke, I., 22
Weber, M., 77
Wengeler, M., 108
Wetherell, M., 12, 14, 131
Wickham, G., 48–9
Widdowson, H.G., 12, 18, 23
Wittgenstein, L., 3–4, 26
Wodak, R., 11–13, 22, 24–7
Wundrak, R., 66
Wuthnow, R., 33, 41–2

Zimmermann, J., 23